How to Analyze People

How to Read and Influence People with the Ultimate Guide to Reading Body Language and Nonverbal Communication

Tony Brain

© **Copyright 2019 Tony Brain - All rights reserved.**

No part of this guide may be reproduced in any form without permission in writing from the publisher except in the case of brief quotations embodied in critical articles or reviews.

Legal & Disclaimer

The information contained in this book and its contents is not designed to replace or take the place of any form of medical or professional advice; and is not meant to replace the need for independent medical, financial, legal or other professional advice or services, as may be required. The content and information in this book has been provided for educational and entertainment purposes only.

The content and information contained in this book has been compiled from sources deemed reliable, and it is accurate to the best of the Author's knowledge, information and belief. However, the Author cannot guarantee its accuracy and validity and cannot be held liable for any errors and/or omissions. Further, changes are periodically made to this book as and when needed. Where appropriate and/or necessary, you must consult a professional (including but not limited to your doctor, attorney, financial advisor or such other professional advisor) before using any of the suggested remedies, techniques, or information in this book.

Upon using the contents and information contained in this book, you agree to hold harmless the Author from and against any damages, costs, and expenses, including any legal fees potentially resulting from the application of any of the information provided by this book. This disclaimer applies to any loss, damages or injury caused by the use and application, whether directly or indirectly, of any advice or information presented, whether for breach of contract, tort, negligence, personal injury, criminal intent, or under any other cause of action.

You agree to accept all risks of using the information presented inside this book.

You agree that by continuing to read this book, where appropriate and/or necessary, you shall consult a professional (including but not limited to your doctor, attorney, or financial advisor or such other advisor as needed) before using any of the suggested remedies, techniques, or information in this book.

Table of Contents

Introduction 9

Chapter One: Reading People Through Their Handwriting 17
- Reading Letters of the Alphabet 18
- Cursive Writing 21
- Letter Size 23
- Gaps Between Text 23
- Letter Shapes 24
- Page Margin 24
- Slant Writing 25
- Writing Pressure 26
- Signature 27
- Stand Out Writing 28
- Concluding 29

Chapter Two: Uncovering Insights About Values ... 31
- Watch for Hot Buttons 32
- Generational Differences 32
- Power and Authority 34
- Individual's Contact List 35
- Language 36
- Reaction to Criticism 39
- How Do They Spend Their Money and Time? 40
- Gut Feeling 41
- A Person's Negative Reaction 42

Chapter Three: Analyzing People Through Their Environment 43

- The Closet 44
- Colors 48
- Prints and Designs 50
- Old Stuff 52

Chapter Four: Judging by the Cover 55

- Good Influencers and Negotiators 58
- Introverts and Extroverts 59
- Reading People Through Their Clothes 62

Chapter Five: Reading People Through Their Photographs 65

- Do Not Rush 67
- Subjective Reactions 68
- Facial Expressions 70
- Relationships 71
- Profile Pictures and Personality Traits 74

Chapter Six: Identifying Deception Through Nonverbal Clues 79

1. Head Movements 80
2. The Direction of Eye Movements 81
3. The Projection Technique 83
4. Nervousness 83
5. Watch Out for Verbal Signals 85
6. Physiological Effects 88
7. The Face Touch 89

    8. How Are the Hands Positioned? 90

    9. The Voice Raise 90

    10. Confidence Variance 91

    11. Observe Person's Shoulders 92

    12. Microexpressions 93

Chapter Seven: Body Language of Attraction 95

    The Attraction Signals 97

    Touch 99

    Mirroring 101

Chapter Eight: Ultimate Nonverbal Clue Cheat Sheet 103

    1. Look for a Clusters of Clues 106

    2. Establish a Baseline 108

    3. Body Language Cues 110

    4. Touchy Tales 111

    5. Tone Tell Anyone 113

    6. The Cultural Context 115

    7. Identifying Deception 117

    8. Nonverbal Cues on a Date 121

    9. Eye Contact 123

    10. Proxemics 125

    11. Mirroring 126

Chapter Nine: Communication to Read People 129

    Talking Too Much 133

    Verbal Modeling 134

Acknowledgment 135
Paraverbal Clues 136
Word Clues... 137
Incongruence in Verbal and Non Verbal Cues 138
Pay Attention to the Emphasis 139

Chapter Ten: Effective Tips and Tricks for Reading People... 143

Chapter Eleven: Personality and Birth Order 159
Why Does Birth Order Impact Our Personality? .. 160
The First Born 163
The Middle Born 164
Youngest Child 166
The Lone Rangers 168
Is It Always True? 168
Factors Impacting This Structure 171
The Natural Elements *171*
Gender *171*
Communicating With People Based on Their Birth Order 172
First Born *172*
Middle Borns *173*
Last Borns *175*

Chapter Twelve: Body Language Reading Tips To Slay Your Next Negotiation 177
The Handshake 178
Mirroring..179

Head Nodding 180
　　　Nervous Gestures 180
　　　Firm Feet Planting 181
　　　Maintaining Personal Space 181
　　　Look at the Hands 182
　　　Leaning 182
　　　Read Them While Reading the Document 183

Chapter Thirteen: Recognizing Personality Type . 185
　　　Cluster of Clues 187
　　　The Four Temperaments Theory 189
　　　　　The DISC Concept *190*
　　　　　Connecting With Every Personality Type
　　　　　... 196

Conclusion 199

Introduction

There are plenty of advantages to being a people reader. For starters, you can understand a person's emotions/feelings more effectively and adapt your communication to accomplish the most positive outcome.

Imagine possessing the ability to decipher within a couple of meetings if a prospective date has it in him or her to be a supportive, compatible, and inspiring long-term partner. Imagine telling through a potential client's verbal and nonverbal clues if he or she will negotiate on your terms. Imagine being able to decode through a prospective buyer's clues if he or she is likely to buy from you. Is a business associate satisfied with your terms and conditions to go ahead with a deal? Is the salesperson trying to mislead you into buying or are they speaking the truth? Can you read people's reactions to steering the communication in a favorable direction?

This is the power of being able to analyze people's reactions. You can predetermine the outcomes of different communication styles and adapt to the one that suits the other person the most to accomplish a beneficial outcome.

Plenty of conflicts we experience in our daily lives are entrenched in our inability to read or analyze other people accurate. We fail to understand how they are thinking and feeling, which creates misunderstandings. Then again, our inherent insecurities are all rooted in what people think about us. Will my partner cherish my existence in their life? Does he or she value me? Does my manager appreciate my skills? These are the most inherent fears that we operate with. Once we learn to read people, these insecurities and uncertainties don't bog us down.

Knowing how to speed read people accurately is nothing short of a superpower or secret magic weapon. Imagine possessing the superpower to quickly read a person like a book. You will be eliminating tiresome guesswork from relationships and focus on communicating with a person that is most suitable for his or her thoughts, feelings, and personality.

When we learn to become more telepathic and master the knack of reading other people, we can use our cards in a manner that is beneficial for us. You don't have to develop the knack of being an FBI style investigator to analyze people or understand how they think and feel. All you need to do is watch out for verbal and nonverbal clues that the person is constantly giving out to know what they are thinking.

A person is consciously and subconsciously giving out plenty of clues about not just what they are currently thinking and feeling but also their overall personality, ideologies, values, attitude, preferences, and much more. You only have to be perceptive enough to tune in these clues at a subconscious level.

I recently read a piece about how the content you like on Facebook can help determine everything from your sexual preferences to gender to relationship status. Imagine, your social media likes determining your subconscious persona. There are plenty of clues everywhere; you just need to watch out for them.

Even when we don't realize, people are constantly giving away signals about how they are thinking and feeling. When you know exactly what to look for, your intuition, perceptiveness, and subconscious communication increase multi-fold. At times, you don't understand people because you aren't actively tuning in to these signals. People are nothing short of an enigma, and learning to watch out for the right clues allows you to put together the prices of a challenging puzzle.

Our knack for analyzing people influences the manner through which we interact with them. When you understand how a person processes information and emotions, the message can be delivered in a manner that is most beneficial for everyone involved.

According to research conducted by MIT, the other person's body language is an accurate giveaway about the outcomes of the negotiation 80 percent of the time. This implies that the person is offering clues about their inner feelings and thoughts involuntarily almost all the while.

An individual's overall personality is a sum total of several attributes, including beliefs, learned behavior, childhood experiences, gender roles, birth order, peer influence, genetics, environment, and others. All these factors are noticeable in the way people speak and conduct themselves.

While a layperson may view people itching their nose as a seemingly harmless or reflex gesture, a people analyzer will always seek deeper meaning in the action.

For instance, if a person has been confronted with facts where their lies have been called out and they start scratching their nose, he or she may most likely be lying. These gestures happen at such a subconscious level that the person isn't even aware that they are sending out these signals or making these gestures, which makes these verbal and non-clues almost impossible to fake. These gestures are directed by the subconscious mind and are more reflex actions than awareness driven behavior.

Research has it that a person retains around 10 percent of the information imparted verbally, and 20 percent of visually communicated information. However, we remember around 80 percent of the information that is conveyed using a combination of both verbal and non-verbal communication methods. This also means that if you combine both verbal and non-verbal communication clues, your chances of being an effective and persuasive communicator will increase.

Body language along with other non-verbal clues is important when it comes to analyzing people. When a person's non-verbal clues match their verbal clues, it is a sign of confidence, authenticity, trustworthiness, and clarity. On the contrary, if there is a clear mismatch between a person's verbal and nonverbal clues, it can indicate mistrust, deceit, and lies. The person may not be telling the truth or maybe trying to hide something. The lack of non-verbal clues can be an indication that a person is not telling the truth or trying to contrive/manipulate his actions to conceal his or her true feelings and thoughts.

Chapter One: Reading People Through Their Handwriting

"Calligraphy is an art form that uses ink and a brush to express the very souls of words on paper"

- Kaoru Akagawa

Every person's handwriting is known to be as unique as their personality. You can make an in-depth analysis of everything from their behavior to personality to the thought process. Graphology is the science of studying an individual's personality through how they write. Handwriting goes beyond putting a few characters on paper. It is about glimpsing into an individual's mind to decipher what they are thinking and how they are feeling based on their handwriting.

Here are some little-known secrets about speed reading a person through their handwriting.

Reading Letters of the Alphabet

How a person writes his or her letters offers a huge bank of information about their personality, subconscious thoughts, and behavioral characteristics. There are several ways of writing a single letter and every person has their own distinct way of constructing it.

For example, putting a dot on the lower case "I" is an indication of an independent-spirited personality, originality, and creative thinking. These folks are organized, meticulous, and focused on details. If the dot is represented by an entire circle, there are pretty good chances of the person being more childlike and thinking outside the box.

How a person constructs their upper case "I" reveals a lot about how they perceive themselves. Does their "I" feature the same size as the other letters or is it bigger/smaller compared to other letters?

A person who constructs a large "I" is often egoistic, self-centered, overconfident, and even slightly cocky. If the "I" is the size of other letters or even smaller than other letters, the person is more self-assured, positive, and happy by disposition.

Similarly, how people write their lower case "t" offers important clues into their personality. If the "t" is crossed with a long line, it can be an indication of determination, energy, passion, zest, and enthusiasm. On the other hand, a brief line across the "t" reveals a lack of empathy, low interest, and determination. The person doesn't have very strong views about anything and is generally apathetic. If a person crosses their "t" really high, they possess an increased sense of self-worth and generally have ambitious objectives.

Similarly, people who cross their "t" low may suffer from low self-esteem, low confidence and lack of ambition. A person who narrows the loop in lower case "e" is likelier to be uncertain, suspicious, and doubtful of people. There is an amount of skepticism involved that prevents them from being trustful of people. These people tend to have a guarded, stoic, withdrawn, and reticent personality. A wider loop demonstrates a more inclusive and accepting personality. They are open to different experiences, ideas, and perspectives.

Next, if an individual writes their "o" to form a wide circle, they are most likely people who very articulate, expressive, and won't hesitate to share secrets with everyone. Their life is like an open book. On the contrary, a closed "o" reveals that the person has a more private personality and is reticent by nature.

Cursive Writing

Cursive writing gives us clues about people that we may otherwise miss through regular writing. It may offer us a more comprehensive and in-depth analysis of an individual's personality.

How does a person construct their lower case cursive "l?" If it has a narrow loop, the person is mostly feeling stressed, nervous, and anxiety. Again, a wider loop can be a sign that the individual doesn't believe in going by the rule book. There is a tendency to rewrite the rules. They are laidback, low on ambition, and easy-going.

Again, consider the way a person writes cursive "y" to gain more information about their personality. The length and breadth of the letter "y" can be extremely telling. A thinner and slimmer "y" can be an indication of a person who is more selective about their friend circle. On the other hand, a thicker "y" reveals a tendency to get along with different kinds of people. These are social beings who like surrounding themselves with plenty of friends.

A long "y" is an indication for travel, adventure, thrills, and adventures. On the other hand, a brief cursive "y" reflects a need to seek comfort in the familiar. They are most comfortable in their homes and other known territories. A more rounded "s" is a signal of wanting to keep their near and dear ones happy. They'll always want their loved ones to be positive and cheerful.

They will seldom get into confrontations and strive to maintain a more balanced personality. A more tapering "s" indicates a hard-working, curious, and hard-working personality. They are driven by ideas and concepts. Notice how cursive "s" broadens at the lower tip. This can be a strong indication of the person being dissatisfied with their job, interpersonal relationships, and or life in general. They may not pursue their heart's true desires.

Letter Size

This is a primary observation that is used for analyzing a person through their handwriting. Big letters reveal that the person is outgoing, affable, gregarious, and extrovert. They are more social by nature and operate with a mistaken sense of pride. There is a tendency to pretend to be something they aren't. On the contrary, tiny letters can indicate a timid, reticent, introvert, and shy personality. It can indicate deep concentration and diligence. Midsized letters mean that an individual is flexible, adjusting, adaptable, and self-assured.

Gaps Between Text

People who leave a little gap in between letters and words demonstrate a fear of leading a solitary life. These people always like to be surrounded by other folks and often fail to respect the privacy and personal space of other people. People who space out their words/letters are original thinkers and fiercely independent. For them, they place a high premium on freedom and independence. There is little tendency for being overwhelmed by other people's ideas, opinions, and values.

Letter Shapes

Look at the shape of an individual's letters while decoding their personality. If the writing is more rounded and in a looped manner, the person tends to be high on inventiveness and imagination! Pointed letters demonstrate that a person is more aggressive and intelligent. The person is analytical, rational, and a profound thinker. Similarly, if the letters of an alphabet are woven together, the individual is methodical, systematic, and orderly. They will rarely work or live in chaos.

Page Margin

If you thought it's only about writing, think again. Even the amount of space people leave near the edge of the margin determines their personality. Someone who leaves a big gap on the right side of the margin is known to be nervous and apprehensive about the future. People who write all over the page are known to have a mind full of ideas, concepts, and thoughts. They are itching to do several things at once and are constantly buzzing with ideas.

Slant Writing

Some people show a marked tendency for writing with a clear right or left slant while other people write impeccably straight letters. When a person's letters slant towards the right, he or she may be affable, easy-going, good-natured, and generally positive. These people are flexible, open to change, and always keen on building new social connections.

Similarly, people who write slanting letters that lean towards the left are mostly introverts who enjoy their time alone. They aren't very comfortable being in the spotlight and are happy to let others hog the limelight. Straight handwriting indicates rational, level-headed, and balanced thinking. The person is more even-tempered, grounded, and ambivalent.

There is a tiny pointer here to avoid reading people accurately. For left-handed people, the analysis is the opposite. When left-handed people have their letters slanting to the right, they are shy, introverted, and reserved. However, if their letters slant to the left, they may be outgoing, gregarious and social extroverts.

Writing Pressure

The intensity with which an individual writes is also an indicator of their personality. If the handwriting is too intense and full of pressure (there is indentation), the individual may be fiery, aggressive, obstinate, and volatile. They aren't very open to other people's ideas, beliefs, and opinions. There is a tendency to be rigid about their views.

On the contrary, if a person writes with little pressure or intensity, they are likely to be empathetic, sensitive, and considerate towards other people's needs. These people tend to be kind, enthusiastic, passionate, lively, and intense.

Signature

A person's signature reveals plenty about an individual's personality. If it isn't comprehensible, it is a sign that he or she doesn't share too many details about themselves. They fiercely guard their private space and are reticent by nature. On the contrary, a more conspicuous and legible signature is an indication of a self-assured, flexible, transparent, assured, confident, and satisfying personality. They are generally content with what they've accomplished and display a more positive outlook on life.

Some people scrawl their signature quickly, which can be an indication of them being impatient, restless, perpetually in a hurry, and desiring to do multiple things at one time. A carefully written and neatly-organized signature is an indication of the person being diligent, well-organized, and precision-oriented.

Signatures that finish in an upward stroke demonstrate a more confident, fun-loving, ambitious, and goal-oriented personality. These people thrive on challenges and aren't afraid of chasing these dreams. Similarly, signatures that finish with a downward stroke are an indication of a personality that is marked by low self-esteem, lack of self-confidence, low ambition, and a more inhibited personality. These folks are likelier to be bogged down by challenges and may not be too goal-oriented.

Stand Out Writing

If a particular piece of writing stands out from the other text, look at it carefully to understand an individual's personality.

For example, if the text is generally written in a more spread out and huge writing, with only some parts of the text stuck together, the person may most likely to be an uncertain, dishonest, or mistrustful individual, who is trying to conceal some important information.

Concluding

Though studying an individual's handwriting can offer you accurate insights about his or her personality, it isn't completely fool-proof. There are several other factors that are to be taken into consideration to analyze a person accurately. It has its own shortcomings and flaws. At times, people may write in a hurried manner, which can impact their writing. Similarly, the way people construct their resume or application letter may dramatically vary from the manner in which they may write a to-do list or love letter.

If you want an accurate reading of someone's personality, consider different personality analysis methods like reading verbal and non-verbal communication techniques. Various techniques may offer you a highly in-depth, insightful, precise, and comprehensive method of understanding a person's inherent personality.

Chapter Two: Uncovering Insights About Values

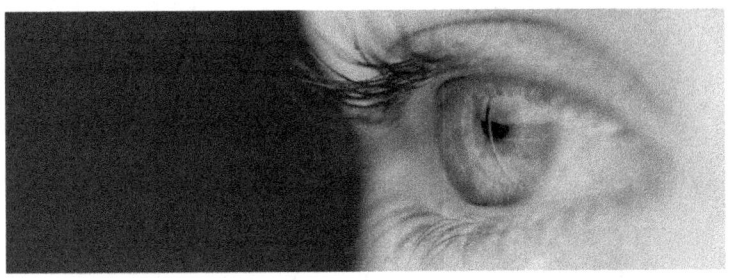

"Don't believe what your eyes are telling you. All they show is limitation. Look with your understanding."

— Richard Bach

Mind reading isn't about drinking some magic potion and developing telepathic powers overnight. It is a science that is carefully nurtured and mastered by people to attain success in their daily lives. Reading or analyzing people is a valuable skill that can come handy in any situation from approaching your manager for a raise to understanding a customer's needs to impressing a prospective date.

Here are some proven tips for deciphering people's values, wishes, and desires through their thoughts, behavior, and actions.

Watch for Hot Buttons

What are the emotional stimulants of a person you are studying? What is their comfort zone? Identifying people's emotional triggers is a great way of gaining insight into their beliefs, value system, and wishes.

A handy tip for learning more about a person's ideologies and values is to pose open-ended questions to them. Rather than asking closed-ended yes/no questions, pose queries that urge them to offer more in-depth responses. This can provide a glimpse into an individual's values.

Generational Differences

Though this is not a 100 percent foolproof method for analyzing a person's values, it can be an effective baseline for reading their personality through the manner in which they view the world.

Generational differences may be more fascinating and insightful than people believe. Millennials focus on establishing more non-personal communication channels through social media or messenger.

On the other hand, Boomers may prefer face to face interactions where they can establish more meaningful and personal connections with others. They seek to set-up relationships where verbal and non-verbal signals are effective to make the most of their communication. Identifying an individual's generation can help to read them or try to establish a favorable rapport with them.

For example, if you want to close the deal with a youngish CEO, you know there are lower chances of them wanting to complete the formalities face to face. They may be people who are comfortable with technology and sending emails back and forth. Their value system or way of working may be more determined by technology than by the old-fashioned route of taking potential clients and business associates on elaborate lunches and dinners. Knowing a person's generation can help you gain insights into another person's values, beliefs, and principles.

Power and Authority

How a person handles power reveals a lot about their values, beliefs, and character. What is the individual's overall attitude towards people who they perceive to be lower in status? How do they treat servers, waiters, and other people who can't do much for them or who we perceive to be beneath us in the status quo?

Listen to them talk to a customer service personnel. How do they air their grievances? What is the person's overall outlook towards animals and children? The way people treat other people who can't return their favors says a lot about their values. Are they generally rude to individuals who aren't as powerful as them? Do they indulge in more magnanimous or selfless acts? This reveals an individual's real colors.

Individual's Contact List

It isn't a secret that a man is known for the company he keeps. One of the best ways for gaining insights into a person's value system and needs is through their friend circle. Are they with the same set of people for the last few years? Are they the leaders or followers within their social circle? Do they influence other people or are they influenced by the decisions and tastes of others? What are the types of people they dislike and like?

When you want to know more about someone's values, attitude, beliefs, and principles, ask them about the type of people they avoid. This is brilliant to know their ideologies. They will always avoid people whose values clash with theirs. For example, when people I pose this question to tell me that they avoid people who are high-handed or deceitful, it is evident that they are more drawn towards honest and down to earth folks. Similarly, a person who says he/she doesn't like to mingle with people who are always partying may be more focused, goal-oriented, and hard working. They are hard-working and want to achieve a lot in life.

If you notice carefully, you will identify a clear pattern in everyone they avoid. These traits reveal their own set of values. For example, sometimes you will notice that you just won't like certain people or you may subconscious avoid them. On closer scrutiny, you'll realize that they may all be ineffective listeners who do not show consideration for other people's thoughts, opinions, beliefs, and feelings.

They may be more focused on being heard and putting their point across than listening to others. All this will help you realize that people who dislike or avoid such people may boast of a more empathetic personality that places a high premium on tuning in to other people's emotions.

Language

A person's beliefs, values, desires, and principles are to a large extent revealed by their words.

According to psychologists, we tend to emphasize on adjectives than pronouns while speaking, which offers subconscious indications of our persona. A high number of personal pronouns demonstrate an egocentric, selfish, and self-centered personality. It can also be an indication of increased self-awareness, honesty, and integrity.

There are other things that determine an individual's personality. For example, if a person is using big words or fancy terms to expresses their point of view, he or she may possess a desire to be constantly accepted or validates by others. There is a strong tendency to fit in or impress others. The individual may have faced rejection during their childhood, which led them to develop low self-confidence, low self-esteem, and feeling of never being good enough.

On the other hand, people who use simpler words and phrases to express themselves are logical, self-assured, and rational people who are confident of their abilities. They don't seek acceptance or validation from others and are fairly firm in their decision making. People who use words such as "but", "except" and "without" are mostly honest and truthful people who won't hesitate to share details.

Notice how people who are mostly happy, positive, and content do not use "I" often. Similarly, usage of "he", "they" "she" etc. are more focused on others. They place the other person first in a relationship while their own needs are put on the backburner. Even the kind of humor and jokes a person shares can tell a lot about their values, character, personality, and attitude.

Don't we all love celebrities to engage in self-deprecating humor? Or for that matter anyone who cracks jokes about themselves! It is a sign of high confidence, self-assuredness, and self-esteem. These people are confident and secure enough to poke fun at themselves. They don't think or care much about the opinion other people hold of them, which makes them take potshots at themselves freely.

On the other hand, people who are quickly offended by jokes directed towards them may not have very high self-esteem or may be suffering from an inferiority complex. A deep-seated feeling of insecurity or an inferiority complex makes them easily offended by jokes directed towards them. Thus a person's approach to humor along with the language they use can offer plenty of insights into their value system.

Reaction to Criticism

How a person responds to criticism reveals plenty about their values. What is a person's reaction to facing criticism? Do they get defensive, angry, and foul-mouthed? Do they fly into a quick fit of rage? Do they accept their shortcomings with grace? People who handle criticism with graceful are more confident, self-assured, frank, and forthcoming! They aren't egoistic by nature and consciously work on their limitations.

On the contrary, people who don't take criticism too well may most likely be suffering from an inferiority complex, low self-esteem, and inflated ego issues. They may need constant validation and appreciation. In their eyes, they can seldom be wrong. These folks may suffer from a high sense of self-entitlement or a misplaced sense of self-importance. They tend to be egoistic, self-centered, and selfish by nature, which means you'll have to employ a lot of tact and diplomacy while dealing with these people.

How Do They Spend Their Money and Time?

Time and money are some of the most important resources of a person's life and the manner in which he or she utilizes these precious resources says a lot about their values. Do people spend a lot of time and money on building a solid long-term future for themselves of their loved ones? Do they focus on the acquisition of knowledge, learning, classes, skills, and education?

Do they utilize their free time for upgrading their skills or waste it on frivolous pursuits? What are their pursuits, interests, and hobbies? Don't scan people's expenses with a magnifying glass now. All you need to do is observe how people use their valuable

Gut Feeling

We can master all the people analyzing methods of the world and still rely on our gut feeling when it comes to reading people. If you have a specifically terrible feeling about someone and can't peg it to logical thought, it may be an instinctive or gut feeling.

If you think your intuition or gut feeling isn't rooted in a scientific process, think again. What is termed a scientific process is closely connected to the limbic brain. It is a reaction to subconscious clues that the conscious mind has missed. If you develop a feeling that something or someone isn't right, your gut feeling may be bang on.

A Person's Negative Reaction

How a person reacts to someone who refuses their request says a lot about them. Are they respectful and graceful in the face of rejection? Do they accept it graciously? Do they respond in a more violent, aggressive, and volatile manner? Do they respect people's wishes and boundaries? Does the person manipulate people into turning their no into a yes? How a person reacts to refusals can speak volumes about their values and character.

Chapter Three: Analyzing People Through Their Environment

"Joy in looking and comprehending is nature's most beautiful gift"

— Albert Einstein

An individual's immediate environment can speak a lot about their personality, thought process, behavioral traits, and values. Of course, this isn't a pop psychology quiz that pops on your social media timeline every now and then about your hairstyling preferences and nail paint colors determining your personality. These are solid, proven, and scientific methods for making an educated guess about people through their immediate environment or the manner in which they live. There are clear psychological concepts and principles based on which you can tell a lot about a person through their environment. Here are some fabulous tips for analyzing a person through their surroundings.

The Closet

The mess within your physical environment is indicative of the chaos in the mind. This isn't about judging people through their environment; it is about analyzing people through their thought-driven actions. It is reading a person through their thoughts, which eventually leads to the creation of the immediate environment.

A well-organized, efficient, and systematic work station or desk is indicative of clear thoughts, clarity of decisions, good time management skills, and a need to get things done. The person is more goal-driven and is driven by a desire to take up challenging tasks.

On the contrary, a messy, unclean, and disorganized desk can be an indication of a chaotic mind that is filled with nervous and anxious thoughts. These people may suffer from low self-esteem, low self-confidence, and other issues. It can also be observed that excessive cleanliness can be a sign of mental disorders like obsessive-compulsive disorder, and reveal a more nervous or anxious mind that is filled with uncertainties and low self-esteem. There is an obsessive need to keep spaces clean and organized, which reveals a sense of inadequacy and disorderliness in the mind. The person may be trying to compensate for something they believe they lack by keeping their surroundings extra clean.

What is the first thing you think when you see a disorderly work or home space? Again, this isn't about being judgmental but reading or analyzing people through their immediate environment and setting. A cluttered space is often an indication of a cluttered mind. It can also mean that the person is a multi-tasker, who is keen on getting several things at a time. People who are busy or engaged in multiple activities seldom have the time or energy to organize their workspace. As a result, it is left unattended or in complete disarray. At times, a disorganized space can signal a plain lazy personality that reveals a lack of goals and clarity in life.

Again, you'd need to know more y digging a little deep rather than making sweeping judgments based on the space alone. It has been noticed that folks with a gregarious and social personality thrive in chaos around them. Peek into their drawers and they are most likely kept in a disorganized and predictably messy manner. They aren't inward driven or believe in giving time to reflection, thoughts, and organizing their space.

Introverts, on the other hand, are more reflective and contemplative by nature. Since they are inward-directed, a lot of their time is spent in diligently organizing, arranging, managing, and prioritizing their things. These things give them more clarity of thought and ideas upon reflection. Most people, however fastidious about cleanliness, have concealed spaces that are a complete mess.

These are generally areas that aren't frequently accessed. If these inaccessible areas are kept sparkling clean too, the person is most often suffering from deep-seated anxiety of nervousness disorder. These people are generally control freaks who are obsessed with the idea of controlling things around them to an unhealthy level.

Research also reveals that a disorganized, chaotic, and unclean environment indicates creativity and innovativeness. People living or working in such messy and disorganized conditions tend to generate forward-thinking, resourceful, and path-breaking solutions. Yes, the cliché about a scientist, writer or artist sporting a messier look and unkempt hair may actually be true from a personality-psychological angle.

Colors

What do colors within a person's immediate space reveal about him or her? The first thing that people probably look at when they enter someone's home or office is the color scheme used to do up space. Bright, dazzling, and bold colors instantly draw our attention to space while cool colors create a softer and tranquil atmosphere. An individual's color choice can demonstrate a lot about their personality. For example, if the person has an inherent penchant or bold and vivid colors like red, purple, orange, magenta, and others, they may be more adventurous, experimental, and risk-taking by nature. They aren't shy of expressing their thoughts and are constantly seeking new experiences. It signifies an outgoing, gregarious, unafraid, and bold personality. These people aren't afraid to call a spade a spade.

On the other hand, people opting for cooler and more subtle shades may be reflective, quiet, restrained, and analytical by nature. They are generally deep thinkers, who do not make hasty decisions. Their decisions are made after considering all possible options.

People who are inward-focused will most likely have their homes done up in soft, subtle and solid hues, marked by muted patterns. Extroverts, on the other hand, tend to opt for more old, vibrant, and experimental prints. Since they are more social and gregarious by nature, there is an inherent need to impress people. Extroverts are more outwardly focused, which means their decisions are more determined by what they think will please people around them.

Introverts seldom display this need to impress others and will often downplay themselves and their surroundings in a bid to avoid being noticed. Unlike extroverts, they are uncomfortable at the prospect of being the center of attention.

Prints and Designs

It may sound funny (or intriguing if you are like me). However, the prints or designs used to do up a person's home or office décor or even their attire can be very telling about their personality. For example, bright, bold, large and vibrant prints can signify an uninhibited personality that is more self-assured, opinionated, and seldom overwhelmed by other people's opinions. These people are fiercely original in their thoughts, opinions, and actions. They often have their own opinion on multiple issues and are rarely influenced by the thoughts, opinions, and ideas of other people.

Likewise, quirky prints such as graffiti, pop art, animal motifs, and polka dots can reveal a penchant for fun and creativity. It is an indication of a creative, independent thinking, and original personality. The person isn't afraid to express themselves and is least concerned about fitting in with the crowd. They yearn to stand out rather than fit in. These are your path-breakers, rebels, and trend-setters.

Geometric prints can demonstrate an inclination towards order, symmetry, and organization. People who wear a lot of geometric prints or have their homes/offices done up in predominantly geometric prints may reveal an affinity for balance, orderliness, and analysis. There is a deep-seated need to have everything in order.

In an interesting study conducted by Yale researchers, it was revealed that people who spend hours taking showers or in the bath are generally lonely or emotionally deprived people who seek warmth from the bath to compensate for the emotional warmth in their lives. Makes sense, doesn't it?

Do you a wall filled with motivational quotes and inspiring messages in your home or office? You may want to read this then. Psychologists have researched that people having a wall filled with inspirational quotes and messages are more often than not possess neurotic tendencies. These people utilize their environment or the space around them for soothing their nerves and helping them navigate the storms in their lives. Of course, don't automatically assume that something is not quite normal about a person when you spot a wall filled with motivational posters. The best way to gather more clues is to talk to the person. Observe verbal and non-verbal clues carefully to gain deeper insights into their personality.

Old Stuff

Ever noticed how some people's homes resemble a junkyard because they store all the old and unwanted stuff? There are old uniforms, sports jerseys they've long outgrown, clothes that don't fit them any longer and other memorabilia that has no place in their current lives. These are most likely folks who are unable to discard their past and move on. They are unable to let go of the past and move ahead. There is a need to cling on to the past and a refusal to look into the future. Hoarding objects may mean that they are still emotionally connected with memories attached to these belongings.

For example, if you are still holding on to a dress that you've long outgrown because it was gifted to you by a former lover, you are probably unwilling to come to terms with the fact that the relationship is over. You are still emotionally clinging on to the relationship instead of moving on and looking into the future. There is a tendency to be closely attached to people and memories that these objects represent at a subconscious level.

Chapter Four: Judging by the Cover

"Form is everything. It is the secret of life"

- Oscar Wilde

When you walk into a book store, how do you judge which book to pick up and which to pass? If you are like me, you are guilty of picking up books that have fancy titles, attractive covers and lots of visually arresting features. Accuse me of being shallow, but I also look at the quality of the paper. Yes, judging a book by its cover is something we've all done at some point or the other.

We've all been fed on the belief that judging a book y its cover is not the right way to do it. However, in a time and attention pressed world, where we rarely have the time to read people comprehensively, we seldom have an option but to analyze and speed people to make quick decisions about them. Reading a book by its cover or speed reading people may not be such a bad thing in today's times. People's outer appearances can often help you make solid and reliable conclusions about their personality. The subconscious visual that you form about an individual through their appearance is often accurate.

I know plenty of psychologists who believe that making snap judgments about people based on their appearances is an extremely narrow way of looking at it. However, the way a person treats himself or herself just as he/she treats his/her immediate environment can reveal a lot about their inherent personality. It can help you gain a deeper understanding of their personality to make communication even more meaningful.

The way a person dresses or maintains their outer appearance can reveal a lot about their internal feelings. Their exterior can often be a near accurate indicator of their thoughts, emotions, and feelings. Ever noticed how when you are completely dejected or sad, you don't bother about how your hair or face looks? You don't have the inclination or zest to look good.

Similarly, when you are feeling more positive and upbeat, you will invest extra effort in looking good and feeling wonderful about yourself. People are well-dresses or sport a neatly-groomed appearance to gain respect or validation from others. They may want people to perceive them in a more positive light. It can also be a sign of high self-confidence, power, and authority. People in positions of power and authority may also be wealthy, which gives them the resources to be expensively dressed and groomed. It can be a sign of influence, power, and confidence. These folks are viewed in a more positive or flattering light by other people.

Here are some tips for reading people through their cover or outer appearance to make a near-accurate analysis of their personality or behavioral characteristics.

Good Influencers and Negotiators

Imagine a scenario where a plain-looking person is selling you something you don't really need. He/she is plain looking and not very attractively dressed or groomed. Would you buy from him or her? The person doesn't appear like they are in a commanding or influential position when it comes to negotiations.

Now imagine another scenario where an extremely attractive, well-dressed, and nattily groomed salesperson walks up to you and introduces themselves to you. Again, you don't really need what they are selling but you still listen to everything because the person is cute-looking, friendly, and speaks with oodles of charm. By the end of their sales pitch, you realize that you can, in fact, use the product they are selling.

Attractive and well-groomed people have the power to influence people's decisions, however hollow it may seem. Of course, it isn't simply about wearing good clothes and looking good and ignoring everything else. There is a natural confidence and ease with which these people operate. Other factors such as friendliness, conversational skills, intelligence, and other things matter, too. This should explain why some people invest a bomb in maintaining their wardrobes and appearance.

Introverts and Extroverts

Extroverts thrive on adventure, new experiences, and risks. Their brains process dopamine starkly different than it is processed in a person who is more inward driven or introverted. These thrill-seekers think fast, act faster and are prone to be more impulsive when it comes to decision making.

They will move and walk fast, which means they are at a greater risk of injuries.

This can be slightly stretched to conclude that people who have more injury scars or casts have higher chances of being extroverts. Their thrill-seeking disposition and brain make them more prone to accidents and injuries. Yes, these are the people who won't think twice before jumping out of a window to escape an adulterous confrontation.

Similarly, while introverts are more likely to observe your shoes and look at your feet while talking, extroverts will look you directly in the eyes while speaking. Since introverts are more inward driven and reflect upon their options before making a decision, they tend to seize/observe people. There is a tendency to look down at a person's feet because of the awkwardness involved in looking away from a person while speaking rather than looking into their eyes. To avoid this uncomfortable situation of looking everywhere around the eyes, introverts will glance at a person's shoes or feet while thinking.

Since extroverts are more outward driven and focused, they will look people in the eyes while talking. There is a tendency to experience rather than think, which means all their efforts are directed towards experiencing or listening to people instead of thinking about what people are talking about. They'll seldom look in different directions (unless they are lying or there's another clear reason for the mismatch in behavior) and will have their eyes firmly fixated on the person they are speaking to.

Blue eyes and light, blonde hair has almost always been closely linked with introversion. However, there isn't a conclusive study to support this view. More than anything, it is a popularly peddled media notion that is completely supported by the Hollywood and Disney brigade.

There is a definite bias towards light eyes and hair each time a character has to be represented as an introvert. Ariel, Belle, and Hercules are all Disney characters who've been portrayed as introverts with light hair and eyes. Today, you can't go about judging people's personalities through the color of their eyes or hair because people are dying their hair and changing colored contact lenses faster than you can say personality.

Reading People Through Their Clothes

Like we discussed earlier, the manner in which a person dresses reveals a lot about their personality. Neatly dressed and groomed people may have an inherent need to be respected and accepted within their social group. They may have a deep need to fit in or be validated by others. At times, dressing excessively well or paying too much attention to one's appearance can be a sign of narcissism or self-obsession. The person may also be suffering from a deeply-rooted inferiority complex or low self-esteem that they are trying to compensate for by dressing well.

Sometimes, people who pay too much attention to their grooming and appearance may believe that they aren't good enough for anything and may use their looks to cover up for the perceived inadequacies in their life.

One of my friends could never match up to her older sibling when it came to intelligence, social skills, and talent. While the parents lavishly praised her older sister for being an intelligent and talented student, she (the younger sibling) wasn't believed to be striking or extraordinary in anything. Throughout her growing up years, she believed she wasn't good at anything and sought constant validation from people through her looks and clothes. She became obsessed with her appearance and spent huge sums of money on grooming, beauty products, beauty treatments, and makeovers.

Thus, an excessive need to look good and dress well can also be a clue to an inferiority complex marked personality. Know more about a person before you make snap judgments about their outer appearance. However, appearance along with other nonverbal clues can offer you plenty of insights about an individual's subconscious thoughts, feelings, and preferences.

Chapter Five: Reading People Through Their Photographs

"The camera is an instrument that teaches people how to see without a camera"

- Dorothea Lange

There are no escaping people's pictures in the age of a constantly buzzing social media feed. Like it or hate it, people are going to pictures of themselves. However, the good news from the perspective of a person analyzer is you can gather plenty of clues for speed reading people even before you meet them simply by learning to read their photographs.

Imagine gaining some clues about a prospective employee before they come down for a face or face interview or learning more about a client before negotiating an important deal with them. How about picking the right date by gather insights about his or her personality through their social media images? Every image of a person holds a fascinating amount of information, meaning, and an indication of his or her emotional state. We only have to be perceptive enough to watch out for these clues. Sometimes, we are so overcome by the aesthetics of the image or the photography that we completely miss the emotions behind the image.

This chapter attempts to offer you some insights about how people's photographs can be used for interpreting their values, personality, and behavioral traits. There are some obvious and some subtle pointers about decoding an individual's personality through their photos. You'll learn to find more meaning and context within the images rather than viewing them as random shots.

Do Not Rush

Since photographs capture moments where time freezes, you need to study the image carefully to avoid any biases or inaccurate readings about something that may have happened in a microsecond. This may be contrary to the fast-speed, short span of attention, limited energy, and the multi-tasking disposition we display. Hit the brain's pause button, do some deep breathing and get yourself into slow motion before you begin analyzing people through their images. You need to approach the art of analyzing people with both curiosity and compassion.

Don't leave out any details Look at the entire image. What is it that holds your attention when you first look at the picture? What are the conspicuous aspects of the image? Slowly move your attention and awareness to the other parts of the images. Look at it from different angles and perspectives.

Pull the image closer to your vision to detect elements that would otherwise go unnoticed. There are plenty of subtle details that your eye may miss if you don't view it closely. Turning the image upside down or sideways allows you to view it from an unusual perspective, which can change your entire viewpoint about the image. You'll end up noticing things you wouldn't have otherwise noticed.

Subjective Reactions

What is it that strikes you the most about an image when you see it for the first time? What emotions, feelings, thoughts, and sensations overcome your mind when you look at the image on an instinctive level? Think of a single descriptive word or phrase as a caption or title for the image that captures your spontaneous reaction to the image.

Do you think the picture represents pride, anger, anxiety, relief, frustration, confinement, exhaustion, success, elation, exhilaration, smoothness, rage, sadness, and other compelling emotions? Your gut-level reaction offers a clue on what you are thinking about the person.

While observing or analyzing people through their photographs, one of the most important considerations is your instant or immediate reaction. However, you'll need to go beyond the first impression. You'll have to apply some amount of free association to analyze the person. Through free association, you are focusing on all elements of the image. Here are some questions you can ask yourself to facilitate greater free association to analyze people through images.

What does the picture remind you of?

What is the predominant emotion expressed by the person in the image?

What memories, incidents, and experiences can you pull out from your own state of awareness on looking at the image?

How would you title the image?

However, when you are analyzing people through their pictures, beware against what psychologists terms projection. Projection is an unconscious process through which our own feelings, emotions, experiences, and memories distort our perception of other people we are analyzing. You may invariably end up projecting your own feelings and experiences to them than trying to identify their personality. This is especially true for more ambiguous images. You don't know if you are rightly empathizing with people reading them correctly or simply recalling your own experiences.

Sometimes, our own subjective reactions get in the way of reading people accurately. However, overcome this tricky situation and identifying when your own experiences and biases are getting in the way of analyzing people will help you be a more effective people analyzer.

Facial Expressions

Human beings are innately expressive when it comes to tuning in to other people's facial expressions. What is your first reaction on looking at the person's face in the photograph? Psychologists have recognized seven basic emotions in a person – surprise, contempt, fear, sadness, anger, disgust and happiness. Keep these seven basic emotions in mind while analyzing people's expressions in images. At times, the expressions are underplayed or subtle, which makes it challenging to pin down the basic emotion.

Look for pictures where the person may not be aware that they are being clicked since that can be a more accurate representation of their subconscious mind.

Relationships

Again, you can tell a lot about the relationship between people by looking at their photographs. If a person is leaning in the direction of another person, there may be attraction or affection between the people. Similarly, if people are leaning in the opposite direction from each other, the relationship may lack warmth. If you notice a person clinging on to their partner's arm in almost every photograph, he or she may most likely be insecure about losing their partner. It may reveal a deep sense of insecurity or fear of losing their partner.

Try to predict the relationship between people through their body language in images. This can also be done in any public place where you have some time at hand to check people's body language, relationship equation, and reactions. What are their feelings, emotions, thoughts, and attitudes towards each other? Is there a pattern in the manner through which people touch, lean towards each other or look at one another? Does their body language reveal a lack of connectedness?

One of my favorite pastimes when it comes to analyzing people is looking at the photographs of celebrity couples and trying to read the nature of their relationship and/or their personality through their body language and expressions. I try to analyze if the image reveals intimacy, affection, and positivity? Or it demonstrates tension, disharmony, and conflict? Akeret, a well-known psychologist, believes that a photograph can also predict a relationships' future.

Some signs of comfort include smiling, holding hands, titling head in the direction of their partner. Hip to hip posture may indicate things are going great between the couple. How is the palmer touch? If it is touching with the full hand, the partners are close and affectionate. On the other hand, fingertips or fist touching can be a sign of being distant and reserved. Crossing legs may mean that they weren't very comfortable or open at the time the picture was taken. If you find a person crossing their arms or legs in almost every photograph, they may be suspicious, doubtful, cynical, and unenthusiastic by nature.

Profile Pictures and Personality Traits

A big body of research suggests that human beings have the tendency to assess one another's personality through a quick glimpse. This is exactly why first impressions are so lasting. It takes us only three to four seconds to form an impression about a person through their verbal and non-verbal clues. Sometimes, they may not even say anything and we can subconsciously tune in to personality.

A recent research study reveals that you don't even have to meet a person once to form an opinion about him or her. All you need is a quick glance at their Facebook or even Tinder profile picture to gauge their personality. Here are the big five personality traits that are revealed through a person's profile picture.

The big five is pretty much the same to a scientific classification of personalities as Briggs-Myers is for recruitment. This personality approach classifies personalities on the basis of five fundamental traits, namely—introversion-extroversion, agreeableness, open to new experiences, conscientiousness, and neuroticism.

A quick glance at your social media profile picture is sufficient for you to rate people correctly on the five fundamental dimensions. In a research conducted by PsyBlog, it was observed through a scientific analysis of the profile pictures of thousands of social media participant personalities that there were very specific and consistent patterns when it came to each of the five personality attributes.

For example, people scoring high on conscientiousness used images that were natural, filter-free, bright, and vibrant. They were not afraid to express a large number of emotions through their pictures. If fact, they displayed a higher number of emotions through their images than all other personality types.

You'll also find people scoring high on openness taking the most amazing shots. They are creative, innovative, and resourceful. They'll play a lot with applications and filters owing to their creativity. Their pictures will be more artistic, unique, and feature greater contrasts. Generally, people who score high on openness have their face occupy more space than any other feature in the photograph.

Extraversion folks will have perpetually broad smiles plastered on their faces. They will use collages and may surround their profile picture with used vibrant images. On the other hand, simple images with very little color or brightness is a strong indication of neuroticism. These pictures are likely to display a blank expression or in extreme cases may even conceal their face, according to the blog.

Agreeable people may often seem to the nicest people to get along with among all personality types. However turns out, they aren't really great photographers. Agreeable people are known to post unflattering images of themselves! However, even with the poor or unflattering images of themselves, they will be seen smiling or displaying a positive expression. The images will be vibrant, positive, and lively.

Chapter Six: Identifying Deception Through Nonverbal Clues

"The tongue can conceal the truth, but the eyes never!"

— Mikhail Bulgakov

When people used to ask me what is what one superpower I would like to develop, I would always say, the ability to spot liars and cheats. No, I didn't have any super detective or FBI aspirations! All I wanted to do was equip myself to be able to determine when people are lying and when they are telling the truth because this can save us plenty of heartbreaks, relationship troubles, deals gone wrong, and soured social relationships. If there's one superpower that can save you a lot of troubles and conflict, it is the ability to spot lies.

Though we can identify liars on an instinctive level, there are some clear verbal and non-verbal techniques that help you identify deception and lies.

Our unconscious or subconscious mind is capable of detecting liars fairly quickly and accurately. Fortunately, liars offer tons of signals through their words, voice and body language that can be quickly caught by an expert people analyzer. Here are some top tips for making you the ultimate lie detector.

1. Head Movements

People who aren't speaking the truth or trying to deceive others make sudden, unexpected, and erratic head movements when they are confronted with a question. The head will retract slightly and move in a jerkier manner. In some cases, it may tilt a little. This happens in split seconds, just before the person begins to reply to your question.

2. The Direction of Eye Movements

When someone is lying, their eyes will generally move towards their right side. The eyes will go up and then move towards the right. This implies that the person is making up information. Since specific functions are performed by certain parts of our brain, the direction in which a person's eyes move can determine the function performed by their brain.

For example, when a person's eyes move to the upper left, we are most likely trying to recall information that is stored in the memory, which means the person may be telling the truth. However, if a person's eyes move to the upper right, he or she isn't trying to recall or extract information from the memory. They are making up information or lying. When you confront someone with a question, their eye movements will reveal a lot about whether they are lying or speaking the truth. The reverse of this true for left-handed people.

In left-handed people, if the person looks to their upper right while thinking, they are trying to recall information from their memory. However, when they look at the upper left direction when confronted with a question, they are most likely making up facts or misleading you.

So, before you term someone a liar, please ensure you know if the person is left- or right-handed.

But it is not just the direction of a person's eyes. Movements such as raising eyebrows or widening eyes is a non-verbal signal of deceit. People often look and try to pretend they are stunned when their lies are called out. In a bid to appear surprised and shocked at your insinuation, they may widen their eyes or raise their eyebrows. It may be an act to make others feel guilty about accusing them.

3. The Projection Technique

Liars are brilliant at employing the projection technique. When confronted with a question, they will most likely come up with a counter-question after pausing for a while. This is the typical way liars respond. They will pause for a while to buy time, and contemplate their response on being confronted.

This will be followed by an accusatory question directed towards you such as, "Do you think I am a liar?" or "How can you accuse me of being a liar?" or "Why were you snooping around?" and other similar accusatory questions that are specifically designed to make you feel guilty about confronting them.

4. Nervousness

However smart deceivers think they are, they offer plenty of clues through their verbal and non-verbal communication. Watch out for their leg and feet movements because that is one of the most neglected parts of the body, while we are interacting or communicating with people.

Liars can manipulate other signals such as maintaining eye contact or keeping a relaxed posture since the fact that people who are speaking the truth always look you in the eye is now common and a widely shared knowledge. They know that looking into a person's eyes while speaking can make them come across as more truthful.

However, some signals such as faking their leg or feet movements don't happen too effectively since these aren't very visible neither are they noticeable areas of the body. This makes manipulating leg or feet movements near impossible. Plus, it happens at such a subconscious level that it is near impossible to fake. When people lie or try to mislead others, their legs (or even feet) start twitching slightly. They may be fidgeting with their clothes or pretend to brush something off from their shoulders.

Shrugging or slouching are other obvious signs of a liar.

5. Watch Out for Verbal Signals

While non-verbal signals can reveal a lot about whether a person is lying or telling the truth, his or her words can also be extremely revealing. People who are lying generally speak using a slower and more spaced out way. There are plenty of pauses that they use for buying time.

Their speech will most likely have a more uneven or inconsistent pitch. Liars will be more hesitant in the way they speak. Genuine people answer quickly, while false responses come up only after careful consideration of all options. The person will take more time to think about their responses also slow their speech. It takes time to think of appropriate words when you are lying.

Also, people who lie or mislead others have the tendency to detach themselves from the situation. They will deny any responsibility or detach from the occurrence, which simply means, they'll use lesser sentences in the active voice.

They will seldom use sentences that begin with "I" and will often use passive voice or speak in a manner that something happened to them, rather than they did something. Liars will either offer very little details or a lot of details in a bid to cover the fact that they are lying. There is a tendency they will volunteer with plenty of unnecessary details. They'll attempt to throw your questioning in another direction by offering a lot of details, most of which may be irrelevant, just to demonstrate that they are speaking the truth. They hope people will buy their "innocence" if they give long and elaborate answers.

This makes liars use plenty of fluff words and fillers and very little concrete details. They won't offer solid information. Their sentences will be long and yet not offer anything substantial. People who are lying almost always never offer tiny and verifiable details. They will focus more on emotions or how hurt they are or how someone is feeling. The conversation or interaction will be more fraught with an apparent show of emotions rather than verifiable facts. Always confront a liar by asking them specifics, which only someone who is speaking the truth would know.

Even when you spot a clear contradiction in what they are saying and what you know is the truth, let them continue speaking. Give the confidence that you trust their version of what happened and allow them to give you even more clues about their lies. This can be used for confronting them at a later date. Let them go on and on with stories and created versions that will eventually help nail them. The idea is to catch them in their own spun web!

Liars will almost always detach themselves from an occurrence or event and focus on the other person or people. They will rarely use "I" or "me" while constructing their sentences since they are attempting to detach themselves from their falsehood at a subconscious level. They are not recollecting facts from their minds. Rather, they are fabricating lies, which is why they are trying to distance themselves from their version of events. It happens at a very subtle and subconscious level, and they are obviously not aware of it (until they read this book that is!). There is a very strong need to psychologically distance or detach themselves from the situation

6. Physiological Effects

Lying produces plenty of psychological and physiological effects within the human body (which is what is captured by lie detecting machines) such as immediate blood vessel swelling, rapid heart rate, increased palpitations, sweating, the itchy reaction on the skin, and much more. When blood vessels expand or experience swelling, the skin invariably begins to feel scratchy. This is why liars start feeling uncontrollably itchy when they lie. The itchy nose may not be such a myth after all and may have a deep physiological significance when it comes to spotting liars.

7. The Face Touch

The way in which a person touches their face demonstrates whether he or she is lying or speaking the truth. People who are lying will more often than not cover their mouths using their hands. This is a subconscious gesture to prevent spilling out information that they shouldn't or a way for them to suppress the urge of blurting out the truth. When people cover their mouths with their hands, the thumb will most likely be near the cheeks. Some fingers will be spread over the mouth to psychologically cover it up.

Another sign of deception is when liars are confronted with the truth or a question and instead of answering the question, they break into a fake cough bout. This is nothing more than an attempt to buy time for making up tales.

8. How Are the Hands Positioned?

Keeping their hands at the back can be a sign of trying to conceal something. Liars will seldom reveal their palms or make an open palm gesture. People who are transparent, genuine, and speaking the truth will keep their palms wide open, while those who are being deceitful or lying will turn their palms upside down.

It is a subconscious gesture that they have something to hide. Liars will often place their palms in their pockets to avoid revealing them to the other person, which is a near-accurate indication of them wanting to conceal facts.

9. The Voice Raise

When a person's voice rises slightly or starts becoming shakier owing to muscle contraction, the person may be undergoing some form of stress. Their voice inflection may be higher than normal, and there may be palpable tension within the voice. An expert people reader will not miss these clues.

10. Confidence Variance

Carefully observe the variation in a person's confidence when they are confronted with a question or the truth. They may either freeze or become extremely verbose, thus revealing a lack of confidence or control. If you want to get the person to give away more clues about their lies and deceit, employ a technique used by investigators. Rather than making the communication appear like an interrogation, make it more conversational.

Liars more often than not give themselves away completely by being more illogical, sporadic, and erratic in their responses. If you interact with them in a more conversational manner by letting their guards down, they will invariably give themselves away.

11. Observe Person's Shoulders

Sometimes, a person's shoulders diminish or close in while lying. This is the exact opposite of an expanding posture, which indicates power, authority, and self-confidence. By closing in their shoulders, the person is trying to diminish their posture because, subconsciously and consciously, they are too aware that they have done something shameful, which reduces them in stature.

When they know they have done something wrong, the person's confidence invariably reduces. They are almost ashamed of their act, which leads them to form a more diminutive or reduced posture. Liars often conduct themselves with greater vulnerability. There is always fear and insecurity that their lies will be caught, which leads them into hunching posture. When the elbows draw closer together, the individual takes on a posture that makes them look more diminutive in size, which is a sign of low confidence or vulnerability.

12. Microexpressions

Microexpressions occur in split seconds, which makes them tough to fake. It is near impossible to work on or manipulate one's microexpressions even if people can mislead with their regular facial expressions. These happen so fast that there's no way a person can modify them unless he or she is a practiced manipulator who is aware of body language manipulation techniques. Laypeople, however, will seldom be able to fake microexpressions.

When a person isn't speaking the truth, their mouths will become slightly skewed. The eyes will subtly roll right after the person has spoken a lie. This is a near accurate microexpression of spotting deception. Another not so obvious microexpressions are changes in the color of an individual's cheeks, expanded nostrils, increased sweating, lip biting, and quick eye movements in all directions. These are nothing but signals of brain activity when a liar is processing information that isn't true. There are certain reactions in the brain based on the activity that is happening within it. These processes or reactions are closely connected with movements on the face or physiological facial reactions, which leads to microexpressions.

Chapter Seven: Body Language of Attraction

"Listen to the women when she looks at you, not when she talks to you."

— Khalil Gibran

You may be insanely attracted to a person but may not have the courage to ask them out owing to the prospect of facing humiliation and rejection. Imagine how easier things would be if you knew if they are as much into you as you are into them. Think of a situation where you've been set up on a blind date by enthusiastic friends, or you find a date online, and really want to know if they are attracted to you. You may go out on a first date and come back not knowing whether the person really liked you or not!

Wouldn't it be nice if there could be a telepathic way to gauge if a person feels truly attracted to you? How can you figure out if a person is genuinely attracted to you or is being plain nice to you because they don't want to hurt you (yes, we've all been guilty of this.)

Can verbal and non-verbal clues help you establish a potential lover's true feelings, emotions, thoughts, and intentions? Can body language be used for unlocking a person's subconscious mind to tune in to their innermost feelings and thoughts about you? Use these secret attraction clues (that I rarely share with anyone) to help you gain and increase social proof and experience more gratifying and fulfilling relationships.

The Attraction Signals

When an individual is attracted to you, they will transmit plenty of feel-good or positive non-verbal clues for you to tune in to at a subconscious level. To begin with, when a person is deeply attracted to you, their bodies will almost always face you.

Everything from their face, the chest to shoulders and feet will most likely be pointed in your direction. The person will lean closer while speaking or interacting with you in a bid to get closer on a subconscious and emotional level. When they stand at a distance of under four feet away from you, they are keen on entering or personal space or inner circle of friends. They are trying to physically enter your inner zone or personal space to make a place for themselves in it.

If you want to know if a person is keenly into you or interested in you, don't give in to their interest straight away. Rather than facing them, maintain a shoulder to shoulder position. If the person is truly interested in you, he or she will make an effort to win your attraction. Let them know that they have to win your attraction for you to stand facing them or mirror their attraction signals.

Leaning in the direction of a person is almost always a sign of attraction. We subconsciously lean towards people we are attracted to. When a person leans towards you in a group, it is clear that they are interested in you (or what you are speaking). Of course, sometimes a person may be simply keen on listening to what you are saying, in which case, you will have to look at other clues. However, leaning towards a person within a group setting is a subconscious indication that they are drawn towards you.

Another sign of attraction includes seizing a person from up to down, and then down to up. This is a primitive way, yet still practiced, for checking out the sexual potential of a prospective mate.

Together with other clues, uncrossed arms and legs can be a sign of attraction. Similarly, a broad smile, dilated pupils, and open palms can also reveal attraction. Head tilting is another sign of interest and engagement. It signals a person's desire to communicate to you that they are always around for you. Looking at a person in the eye for long while speaking can also be a huge sign of attraction. If you are attracted to a person or want to win their affection, avoid looking over their heads or even all over the place. It reveals a lack of interest and sensitivity, which will not give them the right signal.

Touch

Touch is a clue that an individual is completely comfortable in your presence. They may also be keen or getting to know more about you. They may get flirtatious or hit on you by playfully touching you. Some of the most common initial attractions signals are placing their hand over your hand, brushing their shoulder or leg against your shoulder or leg while talking to you and pretending to touch you accidentally.

If you are confused about how to read a person's touches, observe how they touch another person versus how they touch you. If they are generally touchy-feely with everyone around, it is their baseline personality. However, if they make special exceptions in the manner in which they touch you, it is more often than not, a sign of attraction. If the individual touches more than normal or in a different way, he or she may be attracted to you.

If you are attracted to a person, use body language to your advantage by conveying your feelings through non-verbal signals. Don't distance yourself from the person even if you don't want to send out very obvious signs of attraction. On a subconscious level, they may not realize they are attracted to you. Similarly, don't go all out and make the person step back in discomfort. Maintain a balance. Start with a light or playful tap on the shoulder or elbows. It is harmless yet reveals that a person likes you. Then gradually, move to touch their arm, wrist or back while talking. Make the touch more gradual and subtle so they don't wince or retreat with discomfort.

Mirroring

Mirroring happens at a deeply subconscious level and is one of the most reliable signals of a person's attraction. Watch out for people mirroring your actions. There is either a deep-seated need to be accepted or they are truly attracted to you. Sometimes after you've just met or been introduced to a person at a party, you'll notice that he or she starts mirroring everything from your words to your nods to your hand gestures to expressions.

People who don't know much about reading or analyzing people will often miss these clues. However, on a subconscious level, this is a sign that the person is seeking your acceptance or approval. When you are leaning against the bar, you'll notice a person come up to you and lean in the same position as you before striking up a conversation. They are doing nothing but attempting to mirror your actions in a bid to make you feel that they are one among your kind. People will hold their glass exactly in the manner in which you are holding yours or they may take a sip on their drink right after you do to show you that they are like you. The feeling of affiliating with people on a psychological level drives people to mirror their actions.

Chapter Eight: Ultimate Nonverbal Clue Cheat Sheet

*"To acquire knowledge, one must study;
but to acquire wisdom, one must observe."*
— Marilyn vos Savant

It is often said that people convey much more through what they leave unsaid than what they actually speak. It couldn't be any truer. It is easy to say what we don't really mean, but because that is controlled by our conscious mind. However, it isn't easy to hide nonverbal clues about what we are thinking or feeling because that is more of an automated process, which is governed by our subconscious mind.

Therefore, tuning in to these clues helps us connect with a person's subconscious, which is more challenging for him/her to control and manipulate, unlike words.

When we communicate with people, we are constantly giving and receiving wordless signals. All our nonverbal clues, including our facial expressions, gestures, the tone and pitch of our voice, the speed with which we are talking, gestures, eye contact, proximity to the other person, and much more convey powerful messages even if we aren't aware of it. Often, these messages do not come to a standstill when we stop talking. Even in our silence, they end up communicating a lot.

People have much less control over the nonverbal messages they convey than what they actually speak. Nonverbal communication is more of an instinctive, emotional, and reflex reaction that is more trustworthy than mere words, which can be consciously manipulated at will.

If there is a clear mismatch between what a person says and how he says it, nonverbal communication is generally granted more weight because it is hard to stage-manage.

According to research, people retain about 10 percent of information given orally and about 20 percent of information given visually. However, 80 percent of the information given in combination (oral and visual is retained), which means people who communicate both orally and visually have a higher chance of putting their point across more persuasively and effectively.

Body language and other nonverbal clues are just as important (or in fact more) when it comes to reading and analyzing people. People are capable of retaining what they see more effectively than what they hear, which means if you are looking to analyze a person, pay close attention to their body language and other nonverbal clues.

When nonverbal cues match a person's words, it's a sign of trust, confidence, clarity, and a comfortable rapport. On the other hand, when the non-verbal and verbal cues don't sync, it creates an atmosphere of mistrust, frustration, confusion, and tension.

Why, even lack of clear nonverbal messages is a telltale indication than the person is carefully manipulating his body language in order to hide his real feelings and emotions, which speaks a lot on itself.

Here are some proven tips and powerful guidelines for acing the nonverbal clues games.

1. Look for a Clusters of Clues

One of the biggest mistakes people make while analyzing body language is looking for standalone signs, without viewing a cluster of clues. It works wonderfully for slick poker player flicks, but not in real life. One often has to view a group of signs or actions to come to a reasonable conclusion about a person's feelings or behavior. For instance, a person may be making eye-contact, and you've been trained to believe that making eye contact is a sign of confidence. This means you ignore all other signs such as sweating, constantly touching one's face, etc. that reveal nervousness.

Always look for a cluster of clues rather than a single non-verbal clue. It is easier to manipulate a single clue than a bunch of everything else pointing to a clear thought or behavior pattern.

Spotting one cue shouldn't make you jump to an instant conclusion. For instance, a person may be leaning in the opposite direction from you not because they aren't interested but simply because they are uncomfortable. If you are depending heavily on non-verbal clues, ensure that you spot at least three to four signs pointing to a clear thought process or behavior.

Try and take cues from different non-verbal communication sources. For instance, you may want to collectively analyze someone's tone, facial expressions, posture, hand gestures, etc. to be sure your analysis is accurate. Working in clusters increases your chances of reading an individual's behavior accurately.

2. Establish a Baseline

It is important to have a clear reference or baseline for someone's behavior to analyze them well in general. There will be instances, of course, where you will be meeting and analyzing people for the first time. However, by getting to know someone better personally gives and makes your insights even more powerful. It gives a more well-rounded and wholesome approach to the analysis process.

Let's consider an example. One of your close friends is a very fast-thinking, swift-acting, and fidgety person. He is high on energy and forever bouncing ideas off people. Someone who doesn't know this friend too well, or doesn't have a baseline for judging him will inaccurately interpret his fidgeting as a sign of nervousness.

If you were to spot him on the street as a complete stranger, you'd believe he was nervous as hell. However, since you now have a clear baseline to understand he's hyperactive and excited about everything, you won't wrongly interpret his fidgety ways as nervousness.

Pay close attention to people's behavior all the time to understand their baseline. How do they behave and react in various settings? How is their speech and communication pattern in general? Are they in the habit of looking people in the eye? Does their voice undergo a transformation when they're particularly nervous? How do they react when they are deeply interested in something? How do they communicate when they are preoccupied or disinterested in something? These are critical points when making an effort to read people. It eliminates all the potential fallacies you can make while analyzing people.

When you spot inconsistencies in their regular baseline behavior, it will be easier to tell something is amiss. It will help you keep an eye out for nonverbal communication patterns that are not in sync with their regular behavior.

3. Body Language Cues

Though this is a huge subject by itself that has consumed realms of paper and ink, let's get straight to the most crucial points. An individual's body language can convey a lot about how they think or feel. For instance, leaning forward or towards your direction when you are talking communicates that the person is listening to you keenly, and is interested in what you're speaking.

Similarly, limbs placed at the sides are an indication of being relaxed and in a positive frame of mind. Maintaining eye continuous eye contact is, in general, a sign of confidence, honesty, and positivity.

Similarly crossing limbs while communicating with a person depicts the person is not open to or interested in what you are talking about. They are more shrouded in secrecy and not transparent by nature. Tapping fingers on the table of feet on the ground can be read as a sign of high nervousness. Similarly, when a person looks away while talking, he or she is almost always resorting to some sort of deception or is simply not interested in talking to you.

Crossed arms or legs are like barriers that indicate that the person isn't really in agreement with your ideas or what you are saying. Even if their expressions are pleasant or they are smiling, these physical barrier signs can be revealing. They are psychologically blocked from what you're saying. What makes this or any nonverbal near accurate is that the process doesn't happen intentionally; it is more involuntary.

4. Touchy Tales

Observing how people touch you can give you plenty of insights about their behavior, and how they feel about you in general. Though touch is a tricky one since most people have their own ideas about touches based on their personal bubble. However, like most body language cues, it can give you a good idea about what the other person is thinking or feeling.

A weak handshake, for instance, could indicate uncertainty, hostility, or nervousness. Similarly, the proximity of a person to you while you are speaking is a good indication of their interest in what you are saying or their feelings for you. People often distance themselves from others while talking, when they don't wish to be intimate, affectionate, or vulnerable.

Research by the Income Center for Trade Shows reveals that if you shake hands with an individual, the chances of them remembering you double. People view you as being more friendly, warm, and welcoming when you shake hands with them.

While as a general guideline this is true, also take into consideration a person's baseline behavior. He or she may not be very comfortable being in close physical proximity to people, regardless of the circumstances. Therefore, in such instances, a person maintaining a distance from you doesn't speak as much about you as it does about them.

Famous Hollywood talent scout/agent Irving Paul Lazar is famously quoted as saying that, "I have no contract with my clients. Just a handshake is enough." It speaks volumes about things you can judge about a person from their handshake.

5. Tone Tell Anyone

The tone of an individual's voice can convey heaps about how they are feeling. Listen closely for any inconsistencies in the pitch or tone of a person's voice. Are they coming across as predominantly excited or angry? Are they trying to hide something?

The volume of one's voice is also a reasonably dependable indicator of how a person is feeling. If a person is taking louder or softer than usual, something may be amiss. Closely observe if a person is using more fillers than concrete words and sentences. It may be a huge indicator that they are hiding something, nervous, or trying to simply buy time to fabricate stories.

Sometimes, people's tone conveys very strong emotions that they are trying to hide or not expressing straightaway. For instance, a person may say the sweetest thing to you but the tone can be more sarcastic, caustic, or grudging. These may be the passive-aggressive folks, who feel the need to address people or situations in a less aggressive manner.

Since about 80 percent of our entire message is communicated nonverbally, note other's words to read or analyze them. The meanings of some words can transform entirely when announced differently, thus making voice tone and inflection an important criterion for analyzing a person's behavior.

For instance, something as simple as the way you end a sentence can communicate a lot about how you are feeling. When you end the sentence an elevated note, you're turning a statement to a question, or approaching the statement with an element of suspicion or doubt. This makes a person appear less assured and authoritative than intended.

6. The Cultural Context

Though some body language cues like eye contact and smile are universal, many nonverbal clues have a clear cultural context or baseline. For example, Italian culture involves overtly expressive gestures such as plenty of waving, loud talking, excited voices, and shouting.

In Italian culture, excitement is more conspicuously expressed than, say in the UK. The nonverbal communication pattern is much more upbeat and loud, which can make it hard for the Italians to interpret the behavior of someone coming from a predominantly British or American culture, where the excitement is more subtly expressed. Therefore, viewing things in a cultural backdrop is important, especially if you're involved in doing business or forging political relationships with other cultures.

Even seemingly similar gestures can have an entirely different meaning in another culture. For example, while the thumbs-up sign (yes, the same gesture through which we seek approval and validation on social media) is a symbol of validation in English-speaking nations, it is considered inappropriate in some regions of the Middle East and Greece. Similarly, while making an "o" sign with your forefinger and thumb is signifies OK in English-speaking nations, it is considered a clear threat in Arabic nations.

Personal space is almost sacred in the Western corporate culture, so respecting associates and clients when they put up some barrier (like a bag or purse) is important. The amount of executives and managers who lose out on business deals for not interpreting these clues isn't even funny.

In addition to the cultural context, consider the overall context of the situation or circumstances under which the behavior occurs. Some settings (like a job interview) require a more formal behavior, so sitting in a particular posture or gesticulating in a particular manner should not be misinterpreted. It can simply be attributed to the demands of the situation.

For instance, your body language at a pub when you are out with co-workers on Friday evenings varies considerably from your body language when you're with them at work. Non-verbal signals will vary according to the situation, so try to ensure that when you're analyzing people, you're also taking the situation into consideration. This will prevent you from wrongly reading a person who is spending a relaxed Friday night with co-workers as laidback, non-serious, and disinterested.

7. Identifying Deception

It is both easy and tough to spot deception in a person. Easy if you look for the right cues and know how to probe. It is tough because signs of deception and nervousness often overlap.

However, it's important to read people and know exactly when they aren't speaking the truth.

Typical cues of lying include:

- maintaining minimal eye contact
- constricted pupils
- fingers on the mouth while speaking
- faster than normal eye movements
- the person usually tries to physically turn away from the person they are addressing
- increased breathing rate,
- face and neck region complexion changes
- increased perspiration
- change in the manner of speaking such as stammering, pitch elevation, and clearing throat

When you notice any or all of these signs, don't instantly jump to the conclusion that the person is lying. A majority of these cues can also be signs of nervousness or fear (can be true in situations such as a job interview). If you want to ascertain if a person is lying, simply probe further and ask more questions to give yourself more time to determine the truth based on both verbal and non-verbal clues.

Reading nonverbal cues will vary from person to person. It comes only when you practice people watching and reading body language on the train, airport, and television (by turning off the sound). Closely notice people's actions and reactions.

When you observe them, try to decipher what they're thinking or trying to say. When there is a group of people, try to decode who the influencer or leader of the group is, and get a feel of what they are discussing among themselves.

Even when you don't get an opportunity to gauge whether you are right or wrong in your analysis, you'll still develop a sharp, trained, observational eye, which will come handy while communicating with others.

While watching out for the above-mentioned clues related to deception, it is also important to keep the person's baseline personality in perspective, along with cultural context and their behavior in other settings. Avoid making sweeping conclusions.

Some people are naturally awkward and nervous by nature. They tend to exhibit pretty much of the behavior mentioned above at regular intervals. Therefore, is important to determine how the person normally behaves. If their mannerisms, gestures, and eye movements are always a bit awkward, that's their personality.

Closely observe their body language and eye movements when you know for sure or have already established that they are speaking the truth. Compare or contrast this with their mannerisms when you suspect that they are not telling the truth. When you observe continuous change while making certain statements, you'll quickly gauge whether they are recalling facts/information or simply cooking up stories.

8. Nonverbal Cues on a Date

Assume it is your first date with someone. Can you imagine how incredibly helpful body language can be in helping you gain insights about the person's behavior/personality, which can, in turn, determine if he/she is a good match for you? Obviously, it's not easy reading people on first dates. Everyone's trying to put their best foot forward. You're also trying to be as charismatic as possible while also expressing your interest in listening to what the person is saying. Where is the scope for analysis here?

Pretty much like everything else in life, with a little practice and keen eye, you'll learn to spot the right signals effortlessly, without investing too much time.

It isn't rocket science or anything overly complicated. Just tune in to simple things like how guarded they are with their bodies. Initially, everyone will appear guarded. They will most likely cross their legs or arms and keep a fair physical distance from you. The palms will generally be held facing them. This is reasonable on the first date.

However, as an observer, you'll have to determine if it slowly transforms into a more open, warm, and welcoming during the course of the date as the comfort level between you and the other person increases considerably. By observing their body language, you'll quickly know if they are genuinely interested in what you are saying, and that if they are naturally connecting with you by demonstrating a more open body language.

We have a tendency to mimic or mirror other people's behavior. So if you want the other person to look and feel more relaxed and less tensed, take on a more relaxed posture yourself. They will most likely mirror your actions and match your behavior.

Leave your arms uncrossed, give an honest smile, avoid physically distancing yourself from the date, and reveal your palms. These cues convey that you are warming up to the other person, which will also make him or her comfortable. Of course, the level of comfort will keep fluctuating during the course of the date, and it will be nerve-wracking to maintain a standard demeanor. If you observe that a particular topic is stimulating a particularly negative body language, stop in your tracks and change the subject quickly.

9. Eye Contact

Renowned among lovers all over the planet, Shakespeare wasn't off the mark when he famously quoted that "the eyes are windows of the soul." Indeed, one of the most powerful nonverbal communication tools us eye-contact between two people. Maintaining consistent eye contact between people reveals trust, openness, genuineness, and sincerity.

Little eye contact during negotiation can prevent you from building a good rapport with the other person. If conveys to the other party that you're not being straightforward, are acting evasive, and worse—you aren't honest.

Similarly, analyzing the other person's body language can give you insights into their personality or behavior. Are they avoiding your gaze? Are they acting more shifty and fidgety? They may not be the best people to do business with, in that case.

Again, you need to spot a cluster of clues and not isolated nonverbal clues. Also, look for any inconsistencies in the person's verbal and non-verbal clues. For example, a person may be fidgeting because he is nervous or new at this. He may just be hired to negotiate on behalf of an organization and this may be his first project. When you look for other clues, you'll realize that the person is simply nervous and not necessarily dishonest. It is also natural to shift gaze when a person is involved in deep thinking or information processing.

Too much eye contact can also signify aggression, power, and a more threatening approach. The other person may be trying to intimidate you by maintaining continuous eye contact.

10. Proxemics

Proxemics refers to the subject of personal space maintained between two people when they interact or communicate face to face. How many times have you felt uncomfortable when someone tried to stand too close to you while talking? The person is obviously trying to gain acceptance or validation from you or trying to make it into your inner circle.

Get others to respect your personal space and respect theirs, too. If a person tries to come too physically close to you during negotiations, he may be trying to intimidate you or subconsciously coerce you into accepting his proposal. If you want to test a person's comfort level before making any move, simply stand or sit at a minimum of four feet away from them, and observe them closely to guess their comfort level.

If they look more open and welcoming, you are being invited into their personal space. If their body language is more rigid and closed, give them more time before jumping into their personal space.

11. Mirroring

Mirroring is mimicking or imitating the other person's nonverbal communication patterns subtly. When interacting with people or meeting them for the first time, check if the individual is subconsciously mirroring or mimicking your actions or behavior.

For instance, if you are seated across a table from another person, and suddenly rest your elbow or palm of the table, do they follow suit? Observe closely for about 10-15 seconds to check if they are subconsciously mimicking your actions.

Similarly, when you lift a glass to take a sip of water or drink, does this person follow your actions? If yes, it's good news. If someone is constantly mirroring your body language, they are keen on establishing a warm rapport with you or seeking approval from you. Try adjusting your actions or gestures to observe if the other person follows suit. You'll know soon enough if they are keen on establishing a rapport with you.

Chapter Nine: Communication to Read People

"You don't have to tell me what your limits are when the decisions you make, your actions and body language says it all."
— Marlan Rico Lee

Verbal communication is everything that is conveyed through written and spoken language. On the face of it, it may seem easier to decipher than nonverbal communication; however, people are also experts at faking what they say, so its interpretation becomes slightly tricky and more meaningful only when combined with nonverbal communication.

Sometimes relying only on non-verbal clues can be tricky, and you will need verbal clues to complement the nonverbal clues for gaining a better understanding of someone's exact motives, behavior, or personality. Imagine if you saw a person imitating a bird's flapping movement without knowing the setting or context. How would you interpret it? The person could be playing some game, he could also be demonstrating the movement of birds to someone, he could be drying himself, or he may be living in an altered state of mind where he thinks he's a bird.

There are innumerable interpretations of a person's behavior and movements, which is why you cannot solely rely on nonverbal clues or body language for a comprehensive interpretation of a person's behavior or personality. You also need to probe further and watch out for verbal clues that reveal more about their motives, behavior, and personality.

For instance, a person may not be feeling too positive or upbeat, but may simply say they're not too bad. In this scenario, it is important to watch out for both verbal and nonverbal clues. Their words and the manner in which those words are uttered may point to the fact that they are in fact not too good.

In the above example, if the person says "not too bad," it can be interpreted as they aren't too good either. Of course, the person's regular verbiage and culture will determine how they usually speak, but their selection of words can reveal a lot about how they are feeling.

Let us consider another example. You open a nice new specialty restaurant in the heart of the city and have a steady stream of diners pouring in to try out the new dishes. Since the venture is still in its initial stages, you're eager to obtain feedback from your new customers to work upon areas that need improvement.

You head to a family who has just finished eating their food for their feedback. The woman promptly says, "The soup was good." How would you interpret this? It can mean the soup was exceptionally good. However, there are higher chances that it means that nothing else was noteworthy except the soup.

When you learn to watch out for verbal cues, you're training yourself to read between the lines. People will often not spell out everything. They'll expect you to read their thoughts and feelings based on subtle verbal clues. For instance, don't we all hold a small grudge against people who say, "You're looking good today. " And we're doing the internal eye roll emoji thinking, "Don't I look good every day? Why just today?" Some positive souls will interpret it as this means I am looking exceptionally good today.

There are plenty of hidden clues in what people say; you just have to listen and watch keenly to comprehend the right meaning.

Talking Too Much

Talking too much can be both—a sign of authority, or a sign of trying to evade the real issue. It becomes all the more conspicuous when the conversation is peppered with a lot of fillers (ah, umm, hmm), silences, and repetitions.

People who are trying to hide something or deflecting from the real issue aren't generally very concise in their verbal communication pattern. They try to buy time by hammering the same point repetitively using different words and phrases.

Confident people in positions of authority or leadership seldom talk fast or in an incomprehensible, rambling manner. They spread out their words, their tone is more even, and speak in a clear, audible, and coherent manner.

Similarly, people who are more self-assured, honest, and open will convey things in a more concise, crisp, and unambiguous manner. They may not always use the right words (dependent on language abilities); however, they'll communicate in a more coherent and synchronized manner. Their sentences are less peppered with gap fillers and ambiguous words and phrases that are more open to interpretation.

Verbal Modeling

It is human nature to be drawn to people who are similar to us. We naturally take to people who share the same interests as us, come from a similar cultural background, possess the same attitude as us, and even speak like us.

Therefore, people who are constantly trying to match your words and talking speed may be eagerly looking to be accepted by you or please you. Doesn't this happen during job interviews?

Sometimes the interviewer is talking too fast, and the interviewee, in his attempt to please the interviewer, picks up the same speed or ends up choosing the same words and phrases subconsciously. This is referred to as mirroring in psychological lingo. You are simply mirroring the other person's words, actions, and attitude to impress them or demonstrate that you're just one of them.

Acknowledgment

A person who is keenly listening to you, cares about you, or is interested in listening to you will almost always throw in verbal acknowledgments in the form of "yes", "yeah", "I understand how you feel", "wow", "sure", "really" etc.

These verbal interjections and acknowledgments communicate that the person has heard you out and understood what you're trying to convey. People who are disinterested or don't care about what you're trying to convey will be less likely to come up with acknowledgment words and phrases during the process of the conversation.

Beware if the acknowledgments are too frequent or over the top (if this isn't the person's usual baseline personality); it can be more contrived or fake.

Paraverbal Clues

Since we've already discussed this in the previous chapters, how they are can be abundant scope for misinterpretation while deciphering verbal clues. Paraverbal clues (similar to nonverbal clues) help in adding more authenticity to our analysis.

Paraverbal clues comprise everything from tone to pause between phrases to the speed of one's speech to the volume in which a person speaks.

Fast-paced speeches can reveal a more deceptive, disorganized and uncertain demeanor, which is highlighted by ambiguous words and phrases. An evenly tempered speed can be an indication of self-assuredness, assertiveness, and balance. This person knows exactly what he wants, and is confident and comfortable expressing himself.

Similarly, a high voice volume can indicate authority or leadership. The person is trying to convey that he is in charge of the situation or trying to persuade people to accept his point of view or demanding attention.

There are several other verbal cues you need to watch out for while reading people. For instance, some expressions or sounds are used to complement words to make the message even more effective. Sometimes, the message is too intense to be conveyed only with the help of words, which means you need to watch out for sounds like screaming, laughing, sighing, and moaning to interpret the message accurately.

Word Clues

Notice how people are almost always dropping clues through their words. For instance, imagine a person has just stated that he's won another award. When you pay close attention to the choice of words, you'll realize that the person is trying to convey that he's won an award or several awards prior to this. He wants to ensure that people know he has done well previously too; thus, boosting his image.

This person may be the kind who is constantly seeking validation, appreciation, and adulation from others to boost his self-esteem. He is likelier to be exploited using flattery and ego-boosting praises.

Incongruence in Verbal and Non Verbal Cues

People can say anything they want and they often lie through their teeth because they get away with deception. However, when you spot incongruence in a person's words and body language or expressions, you know something is amiss. For instance, someone is mentioning that they are really fond of someone, and while saying it, they are almost involuntarily shaking their heads.

Notice how people sometimes say something makes them extremely happy, yet while saying it, their expression is painfully somber. This can be revealing. However, don't jump to any conclusion until you are able to gather more information.

Practice your skills by watching chat shows or talks shows by turning the volume down. Try to guess what these people are saying simply by observing their expressions, gestures, and posture. When you're done writing what you think they are saying, watch again. This time turn up the volume and check if their words were congruent to their expressions or body language.

Pay Attention to the Emphasis

You may not be a trained FBI agent but there are still lots of sneaky tricks and clever strategies that can be used to read people accurately. One of the most important verbal communication cues is the word a person emphasizes while speaking. This reveals a lot about what is important to him along with his choice of words.

For example, if your supervisor says, "I've decided to go ahead with this idea," and emphasizes on the word "decided", there's little anyone can do to change his mind. He's conveying he has already made up his mind and that there's no further scope for communication. Words reflect our thoughts and feelings.

The words we use are loaded with meaning, which consciously or subconsciously ends up revealing plenty of underlying emotions. Similarly, the words a person uses can a lot communicate a lot about his personality. It is an indication of a personality that's not impulsive, more thoughtful, and analytical. Look out for words people use (especially action words) while talking to you. It will tell you more than people think they are giving away.

If someone constantly emphasizes the word "hard" in saying, "I worked hard to accomplish this," or it is "hard work", they are most likely goal-oriented folks who love a good challenge and do not like to be given things on a platter. It also suggests that the person is capable of delaying gratification or holding off pleasure until they achieve the results they are after.

If a job application is constantly using the term "hardwork" (yes I know they all do and they lie too, in which case you have to look for a combination of clues to spot inconsistency in their verbal and nonverbal clues), he may be a more goal-oriented and diligent employee, who doesn't shy away from taking up challenges or big responsibilities. He may possess the required determination to finish the given assigned tasks and can be dependable.

However, you have to be careful in situations like interviews where people are aware that their personality, body language, confidence, etc. are being assessed in a more controlled and closed environment. This gives them the ability to manipulate the actions and body language to create the intended impression. However, if you have a trained eye and some practice, you'll quickly detect any inconsistencies.

Chapter Ten: Effective Tips and Tricks for Reading People

"The highest activity a human being can attain is learning for understanding, because to understand is to be free"

- Baruch Spinoza

Now that you've gained some expertise in analyzing people's behavior, let's sweeten the deal and give you even more amazing tips and tricks to read people like books.

Here are 12 amazing strategies that will give you insights into what people are thinking and feeling to help you understand them better and develop even stronger interpersonal relationships.

1. Even seemingly innocuous questions such as, "How are you today?" may be an attempt to establish your baseline thus, setting the stage for further probing and inquires. This technique is typically used by salesmen and business associates. If you're trying to establish someone's baseline, gently probe them about how their day was, or how they are doing today. It opens the gates for further discussion, probing, and negotiation.
Ask more open-ended questions if you want to set an initial baseline for interpreting people.
2. Former FBI agent Navarro offered many effective tips on reading people in *Psychology Today. O*ne of his tips included avoiding vague questions after establishing a baseline. A rambling individual is tough to interpret. Therefore, ask straightforward

questions that have a direct answer, which makes it easier for the questioner to detect deception. Don't look or appear too intrusive. Simply throw a question and observe, minus interruption.

3. Clues that convey discomfort, stress, and distress include a furrowing brow, clenching jaws, compression of lips, and tightening of facial muscles. Similarly, if someone is shutting their eyes for longer than a regular blink or clearing their throat, there's a high chance they're stalling. Leaning away from you or rubbing hands against their thighs or head is also a sign of high stress.

4. Children are brilliant subjects to practice on when it comes to detecting liars. If you're looking for signs to spot a liar, simply observe what children do when they lie. Annie Duke, a renowned professional poker player, and cognitive psychology doctoral

student suggested that kids are an excellent source to pick up cues about deception. Adults pick up deception skills to bolster social interactions and personal relationships, which kids haven't mastered at that stage. Therefore, they are pathetic at lying. Every sign is clearly visible because they aren't yet adept in the art of lying. Therefore, observing clear signs of deception in them gives you the ability to spot the same signs in adults.

This, of course, comes with its own fine print. Some people will be better at lying than others. Those who have mastered the art of deception will obviously be well-versed in hiding signs of untruth.

5. When someone nods excessively or in an exaggerated manner, it means he is simply conveying his anxiety about your opinion of him. The person is also likely to think that you aren't confident about their abilities.

6. Our brains are hard-wired by default to interpret power or authority with the volume of space occupied by someone. For instance, an erect posture with straightened shoulders conveys authority. It communicates that you are occupying the optimum available space.
On the other hand, slouching is occupying less space and presenting yourself in a more collapsing form, thus, demonstrating reduced power. People who maintain a good posture automatically command respect on a subconscious level.
7. Genuine smiles are easy to tell apart from contrived or exaggerated smiles. When a person is genuinely delighted to see you or by the conversation they're having with you, their smile reaches the eye. It also slightly crinkles one's skin to form crow feet. Smile is the single largest arsenal people use to hide their true feelings and thoughts.

If you want to tell whether a person is smiling genuinely, watch out for crinkles near the eye corners or crow's feet on the skin. The smile is most likely a deception in the absence of these signs.

Did you know that a genuine smile is called Duchenne smile? It is believed that a smile can never be faked no matter how hard a person tries. Have you ever wondered why you or someone ends up looking so awkward in pictures? It may appear on the fact that we're smiling, but we're actually only pretending to smile. Since a genuine smile elevates your cheeks a bit, there are bound to be some crows feet, which bundles up just below the eyes. Body language experts say this is tough to fake.

You actually need to experience a happy or joyful emotion to be able to create that expression. When you're not comfortable from within or not experiencing genuinely

happy emotions, the expressions just do not fall into place.
8. Look out for micro expressions. If you observe people closely, you'll notice that their real thoughts or feelings, and not what they're trying to deceptively convey, will be flashed on their face in the form of micro expressions.

   Sometimes, while trying to come across as consoling, they'll quickly let off a smirk that can last 1/15th of a second. This is because their thoughts and expressions are syncing involuntarily for a moment.

   Next time you're traveling by aircraft, notice how flight attendants smile with the help of their mouth but their eyes are blank, and the eyebrows are in a positioned in a scowl when you ask for more drink.

   The truth almost always slips out in the form of these tiny expressions or micro-expressions. While it isn't difficult to fake body language, look out for the not so subliminal cues, which are a clear giveaway. It's pretty much like shooting stars; you've got to see it fast before it disappears.

9. Avoid making assumptions. One of the best tips you can receive while analyzing people is not to make prior assumptions or have any sort of biases or prejudices. Sometimes, we go to analyze people with a clear prejudice and think we've already found what we've been seeking. For example, if you assume (based on prejudices etc) that a person is angry, then all their actions and words will seem like there's a deeply hidden anger within them. You will find only what you are looking for.

For instance, if we go to a person's workplace assuming that he is totally disinterested in the job or dislikes it, we'll assume his concentration or lack of cheery approach as absolute disinterest in the job. He may be strictly trying to focus on his job as opposed to hating it. Not everyone grins and laughs when they are enjoying their work. Sometimes, they are just involved in performing it more diligently.

Another important point is to avoid judging other people's personalities based on your own. For instance, in the above scenario, if you truly love your job, you'd have a more positive, grinning, and happy expression as opposed to a more somber look. However, not everyone shares your unique traits, behavior, attitude, beliefs, and values.

10. Identify behavior patterns. Take for instance you're flying in an aircraft and a particular cabin crew member looks really pissed off while talking to a passenger seated near you. Now, you can quickly jump to the conclusion that he or she has an inherently arrogant, impatient, and hostile personality.

However, he or she may have just fought with his or her partner before boarding the aircraft and may still be carrying the anger within him or her. You really can't tell if it's the former or latter until you observe a clear or repetitive pattern.

Does she look particularly annoyed when passengers ask for something? Well, then you've spotted a pattern. If not, you're just being plain unfair in judging him or her based on a single isolated pattern that originated due to another external situation (argument with her partner.) Looking for patterns helps you analyze people more objectively and accurately.

11. Compare behavior. When you've noticed that someone is behaving particularly out of sync within a group of people or in a specific setting, observe whether they display the same behavior in other groups, too. Also, if someone is acting slightly off the normal course with a person, try and gauge if they repeat the same actions with others, too.

Continue to observe the person's actions in multiple settings to gain a comprehensive insight into his personality or behavior. Does the individual's expression or gestures change? Does his posture undergo a transformation? What about the voice and intonation? These clues help you know if the behavior you observed initially is a norm with them or simply an exception.

12. Notice people's walk. The way a person walks can reveal a lot about him. People who are constantly shuffling along demonstrate a clear lack of coherence of flow in things they take up.

    Similarly, people walking with their heads bowed reveals a lack of self-confidence or self-esteem. If you do observe one of your employees walking with their head down, you may want to help build the person's spirit. Appreciate him more in public and give him tasks that demonstrate your faith in him. Approach him by asking him open-

ended questions during meetings to get him to talk more and bounce ideas off people.
13. Power play with voice. Much as people like to believe, the most powerful or commanding person is not the one at the helm of the table. It is the person with a confident, firm and strong voice. Confidence denotes power.

At any conference table or business lunch, the most powerful and influential/persuasive individual is the one who has a confident and commanding voice, and huge smile (smiling is a sign of effortless confidence almost like the person is so good, he doesn't have to try too hard). However, do not confuse a loud voice with a confident/strong voice. Merely speaking loudly won't earn you respect if you sound shaky and confused.

When you're pitching an idea/product to a group of decision-makers or people in general, watch out for people with the strongest and firmest voice. These are the people the leader may generally rely on for making decisions or these are the group influencers. When you learn to observe and identify the strong voices, your chances of a positive outcome increase drastically. People in power often keep their voice low, relaxed, and maximum pitch. They don't speak in a tone that elevates in the end as if they are asking a question or sounding uncertain/doubtful about something or looking for approval. They will spell their opinion in a more statement like manner by employing a more authoritative tone that elevates in the middle of a sentence, only to drop down in the end.

14. Stand opposite a mirror to observe your own body language. Give yourself various scenarios (party, informal outing with friends, a business presentation) and start talking like you would in these settings.

Being aware and conscious of your own body language in varied settings will help you identify patterns on other's body language too. Not just the mirror, the next time you find yourself at a negation table or first date, try to be more aware of your body language and the impression you are trying to convey. This will help you decipher the other person's thoughts and emotions more effectively through their body language. Observe your own body language without being self-conscious or judgmental. Look how your eyes light up when you are talking about someone you care for deeply. Notice how your eyebrows raise when you are speaking to someone you don't really like or trust. This will help you gain a better understanding of other people's thoughts and feelings.

Notice everything from your eye movements to gestures to posture. This will help you understand exactly what you need to watch out for while analyzing other people.

By tuning into your own underlying feelings and emotions, you will be able to judge other people's body language, words, and actions more accurately.

15. When people try to manage their body language by misleading others, they concentrate on their postures, facial expressions, gestures, and postures. Since their legs movements are more unrehearsed, this is where you're most likely to find deception. When in stress and duress, they will display signs of nervousness, fear, and anxiety with their legs.

    If you watch closely, their feet will fidget, shift, and wrap around each other make increased movements. The feet will involuntarily stretch, kick and curl their feet to eliminate tension.

Research has revealed that people readers will enjoy higher success analyzing a person's emotional state just by observing his or her body. Even though you may not be aware of it until now, you've been intuitively responding to leg and foot gestures all the while.

Chapter Eleven: Personality and Birth Order

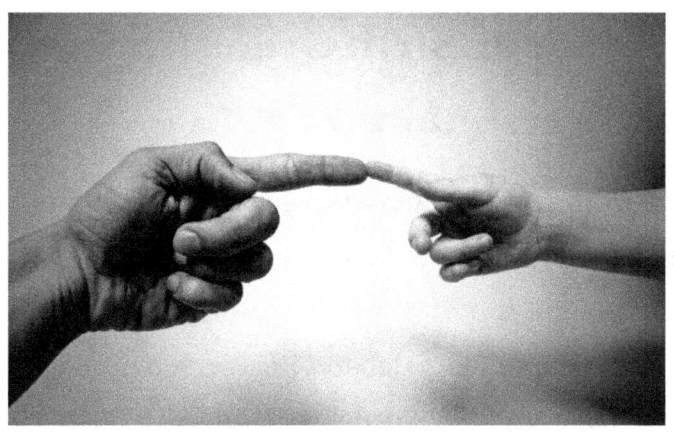

"A brother is a friend given by Nature"

- Jean Baptiste Legouve

Nope, the effect of birth order on personality type is not just pop psychology, BuzzFeed quiz-style talk. It is in fact based on consistent research and scientific principles. Chuck aside the entertainment and stereotypes, and you have a near accurate technique for determining someone's personality. There are plenty of psychological principles behind the amusing stereotypes that determine people's personalities depending on their birth order.

Why Does Birth Order Impact Our Personality?

According to some psychologists, birth order is as crucial as genetics in determining an individual's personality. It boils down to the nature versus nurture personality debate. Research has pointed to the fact that birth order can indeed influence our personality owing to the fact that the way parents relate to every child of theirs (based on his or her order of birth) is different. Children from the same household never assume the same role.

There is always a clear demarcation of roles and equations between the parents and children vary based on their birth order. For instance, if you are the oldest among siblings and assume the role of a caretaking sibling, no one else will fill that role. The others will then pick other roles, says an achiever or provider.

Parents are almost always directed by a different approach at the birth and subsequent upbringing of each child. The firstborn instills a sense of pride and paranoia in parents. If you are a parent, you'll understand how frightened you were at each potential injury of your firstborn. Similarly, the middle born is often bossed over or dominated by the firstborn sibling, who is already sufficiently acquainted with the ways of the world. The older sibling is viewed as wiser, responsible, and competent.

Compared to the firstborn, the other children are less likely to be micro-managed by the parents, thus changing the equation between them slightly. Parents are more exhausted and worn out by the time the later siblings arrive.

They most likely realize that their fears are unfounded and that the baby doesn't really need to be micromanaged. Thus, parents turn slightly more flexible when it comes to disciplining and attending to later children. Therefore, middle and younger siblings learn to attract attention.

It isn't a biological process where just because you jumped out of your mother's tummy first, you are destined to be a leader. Rather, it is about how the parents treated the child depending on this birth order that leads to the child developing a specific personality.

Since the firstborn is more of an experiment for the parents, there is a greater tendency to be overly obsessed with minute details, thus leading the child to be a perfectionist. On the other hand, the youngest born child is born when the parents have already figured things out.

The youngest child is also competing for attention with older siblings, which makes him more of a people please and less obsessed with the idea of perfection.

The First Born

The firstborn child in a household is often believed to be ambitious, dominating, and responsible. They are known to be natural leaders and often lead by example. These are the folks people often look up to for guidance and solutions. They operate with a deep sense of responsibility and are goal-driven.

Since firstborn children enjoy undivided attention, at least for some time from their parents, they are naturally used to being in the front or limelight. They feel like there's no competition and that they are born to lead. It can be seen as a byproduct of the attention showered on them in the absence of other siblings.

The firstborn child may connect more effectively with other firstborns than his or her siblings owing to the birth order. Parents often rely on their firstborns to assist with taking care of their younger siblings, which makes them responsible and reliable.

They are more often than not well-behaved, meticulous, caring, and conscientious. This comes from the idea that others rely on them. From childhood, they've been conditioned to believe that others are dependent on them for support and guidance.

It isn't surprising then that they turn out to be high achievers who constantly seek validation and appreciation from others. They also tend to have a dominating personality and are perfectionists by nature. The older siblings assume the role of a mini parent while also being insecure at the prospect of losing the parents' undivided attention.

The Middle Born

The general notion about middle born children is that they have a high sense of fairness and peace.

Middle children are generally understanding, adjusting, co-operative, yet competitive. They are likely to have a close set of friends, who give them the attention they've not got from the family.

Middle children often receive the least attention and affection from the parents, which makes them turn outside the house for forging more meaningful relationships.

They are generally late bloomers and find their calling after much deliberation and experimentation. However, middle born people are often at the helm of powerful and authoritative careers that let them use their slick negotiation skills. This helps compensate for all the attention they probably didn't get as children.

The personality traits of a middle child are diagrammatically opposite to the characteristics of the first and young child. However, they are unique, juxtaposed between siblings and this role makes them expert negotiators. They quickly learn to navigate their way through tricky and awkward situations. This equips them for entrepreneurship and other positions of authority.

Youngest Child

By the time the youngest child is born, the parents are fairly assured of their expertise as caregivers. They are no longer paranoid or hesitation about their skills as parents. This makes them more flexible and lenient towards the youngest child. There isn't a tendency to monitor every move of the child, which makes more independent. Younger siblings generally enjoy more freedom and thus become independent thinkers and decision-makers. The youngest and oldest children have few traits in common because they've both been brought up with a high sense of self-entitlement.

They've both been made to feel special based on their oldest and youngest positions in the household. Younger siblings have always learned to deal with their parents' divided attention. They are fairly adept at handling competition and aren't bogged by feelings of insecurity and jealousy. They operate with a sense of security and often know their place.

Since the parents are more flexible with them, youngest born people often tend to follow their hearts calling. You will find them in more creatively stimulating professions such as stand-up comedians, actors, painters, writers, and dancers.

The youngest born tends to take more risks, have an untamed spirit, and are often exceedingly charming. If someone tells you they are the youngest sibling in the family, they almost always know how to wriggle out any situation by using their charm. Don't forget to overlook the context though when you're analyzing people.

Sweeping judgments don't work very well when it comes to analyzing people. There may be several things to consider such as situation, setting, context, and culture. In your over-enthusiasm to read people, you may end up making incorrect observations by overlooking context.

The Lone Rangers

Yes, I know what you are wondering. What if you happen to be the only child and don't fit into any order of birth? Lone rangers or the "only child" is often more mature and confident. They tend to think beyond their years owing to the fact the lone rangers are almost always surrounded only by adults in the household. In the absence of siblings, much of their interaction is only with grown-ups of the household.

Having spent a lot of alone time, they become more confident, independent, solution-oriented, creative, and resourceful. Lone rangers have a lot in common with firstborn children. They also share the self-entitlement and feeling of specialness that is associated with the youngest siblings.

Is It Always True?

It may not always be true because parents are known to set extremely high expectations for the firstborn. When first born children do not meet their parent's expectations, they can become highly rebellious. There is a rejection of his or her role.

It is true that most middle born children are excellent peacekeepers and negotiators because they neither have the rights of the oldest sibling nor the special privileges of the youngest sibling. Caught in the middle, they learn to negotiate their way through life and become exceptionally good peacemakers.

They are more emotionally connected to their friends, owing to the fact that they don't receive the desired attention from the family. They tend to become social butterflies who spend more time outside the house.

It is a known fact that parents aren't as stringent or careful about their youngest child since they are fairly experienced in raising children. They have already seen their older children grow with the required trial and error, and are hence more at peace. A majority of the time, parents are more financially independent by the time their youngest child is born. Thus, the overall feeling of contentment, security, and leniency towards them is high.

Sometimes, the youngest children don't fancy being the baby of their household. There is an increased need to be taken more seriously. This drives them to be more serious about their responsibilities.

Always pay close attention to how people refer to their birth order while speaking about it. Do they appear more positive or negative about their position? This reveals a lot about whether their birth order has been a bane or boon while influencing their personality. Similarly, observe people's body language while they are speaking about their birth order.

Factors Impacting This Structure

Birth order is not a precise science for determining an individual's personality. It is a good practice to try and know more about an individual's siblings if you are trying to read their personality based on birth order. In addition to birth order, there are several other determinants of who a person turns out to be.

The Natural Elements

Genetics is the single most influential determinant of an individual's personality. About 50 percent of who we are is determined by our genetic make-up. A majority of our personality is influenced by natural, in-born factors.

Gender

Other than birth order, gender also influences who we become or the roles we assume within our household. For instance, if the firstborn is a son, and the second born is a daughter, they will each have their own gender-based identity.

The daughter will not be bogged down by the pressure of living up to the boy's accomplishments and responsibilities. If the second child was a son, he would've probably experienced the pressure of living up to the older man's achievements. However, since it is a girl, the pressures are not as marked since she will have an identity of her own based on her personality.

Communicating With People Based on Their Birth Order

First Born

Firstborns on account of their undivided attention status, at least for some years, tend to be dominating, leading and controlling by nature. There are in fact two categories of firstborns. The first is the rule-abiding, responsible, and the compliant firstborn type who strives to be an example for their siblings.

The second category is aggressive and dominating leaders who know how to get things done owing to their perfectionist ways. Be a good team player, follow the rules, and demonstrate a caring approach towards the former category. Similarly, seek the expertise, and stick to perfect ways of the second type. The leaders enjoy being in control and issuing instructions, so you need to be a good follower while dealing with them. They derive a great sense of importance when people ask for expertise or guidance.

Middle Borns

Middle borns are often known to be rebellious by nature since they do not enjoy the special privileges of the first and last born. They often do not get the attention enjoyed by the firstborn or the special pampering received by the second born.

Showering them with special attention or offering genuine compliments is a great way to get into their good books. They tend to be either outgoing or lonely. Try to win the confidence of the lonely middleborns without pushing them to open up.

Give them their time and space, and you'll do well. Do not rush them into anything. Similarly, if you're negotiating with them, you better be excellent at the game because middleborns can be exceptionally gifted negotiators.

Handle the rebellious with gentle firmness. Be assertive yet polite while communicating them. They are good at compromising in any situation, which is why they also quickly take to peacemakers and solution providers.

Avoid confrontation and deal with them in a more sensitive, and accommodating manner. Learn to be more compromising and adjusting while dealing with them.

They may have issues with assertiveness, confidence, and self-esteem. Keep this mind while interacting with them. Boost their self-esteem while interacting with them, and you'll win brownie points with them.

Last Borns

Last borns on account of being "the baby of the family" generally become less self-reliant and independent compared to their siblings. They can often be unrelenting and stubborn. The best way to deal with them is to shower them with attention and affection. They are happy to take suggestions and advice because they aren't very independent thinkers. Don't try to negotiate with them as when they make up their mind, they are almost always sure.

Chapter Twelve: Body Language Reading Tips To Slay Your Next Negotiation

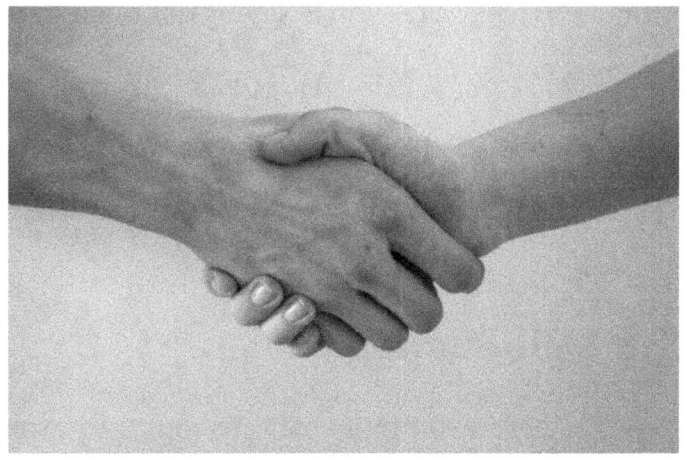

"Information is a negotiator's greatest weapon"

- Victor Kiam

Like any social scenario, you are interacting across verbal and nonverbal channels. It literally results in two simultaneous conversations at one time. According to research, people send more than eight hundred distinct nonverbal clues over half an hour of negotiation.

If you focus only what the person is saying, you are losing out on a whole chunk of the message. Construct a brilliant bargain by understanding by tuning in to what a person is saying consciously as well as subconsciously.

Here are a few tried and tested tips to ace your next negotiation by reading the other person or party accurately.

The Handshake

There have been volumes written about the perfect handshake. A firm handshake on meeting the person or being introduced to him or her is an indication of confidence, self-assuredness, determination, and courage. A business associate or potential client who shakes your firmly is subconsciously trying to convey to you that they are up for the negotiation game and are more or less firm in their decisions. Clutching a person's hand too tightly can be read as a sign of aggression, superiority, power, or intimidation.

On the other hand, a limp handshake symbolizes lack of confidence, low self-esteem, lack of clarity or low determination.

Mirroring

If the other person mirrors your actions, gestures, tone, or words, it is a positive sign they are keen to impress you or buying what you say. The prospect or business associate is most likely engaged. They will lean forward or mimic your movements. When people aren't taking to what you are saying or are switching off, they'll lean back.

Their arms and legs will be crossed. Find a way to draw the person into the conversation and find out why they are closed to what you are saying. Don't go any further when you find a person crossing his arms and legs. Try to get them to uncross their arms and legs or they'll subconsciously not absorb what you are speaking.

Head Nodding

Frequent head nodding is a sign that the other party is eager to gain your acceptance or validation. They are ready to do what you are saying to impress you. A person who maintains eye contact while nodding continuously implies the negotiation is going in the right direction. It is a sign of diffusing hostility or tension and creates a sense of being on the same plane with the other party.

Nervous Gestures

People tend to reveal their stress or nervousness through their hands. Fidgeting, twiddling, or clasping hands is a huge sign of nervousness. If you are trying to make an important or powerful point, keep your hands below the chest. Pull or entwine your fingers to make the point in a more confident and forceful manner.

Firm Feet Planting

Again, the feet are the most non-obvious part of the body while reading a person's body language, which is why we tend to overlook a lot of revealing feet or leg movements. If people's feet are firmly or resolutely placed on the ground, he or she is firm about their point. They are resolute and not likely to change their stance. It is also a sign of high confidence, security, and self-assuredness.

Maintaining Personal Space

As discussed earlier, the field of proxemics involves focusing on the distance between two people while communicating. A person standing too close to you may be attempting to coerce or intimidate you into accepting their point. It can also be a sign of attention and interest.

The feeling of hostility is less marked when the person maintains a minimum distance of four feet from you. It indicates they respect your personal space or are not trying to physically intimidate you. They are giving you an option to make your decision after weighing all facts and figures.

Look at the Hands

Hands are the most expressive parts of our body, which means, it adds plenty to the meaning of the message. As a thumb rule, if the person is rubbing their face, they are generally nervous or anxious. Similarly, when a person is keeping his or her hands on the mouth, they may be lying or concealing some important information. If the person keeps his or her hands away from their face, they are confident and truthful.

Hands left loosely in a relaxed position at the side of the body is a positive sign that the person is comfortable about what is being said. They are listening to you in a relaxed and positive manner.

Leaning

If a person has an open posture and leans in your direction, he or she is keenly listening to or interested in what you are saying. They are also interested in knowing your opinion or take on the points they have presented.

Read Them While Reading the Document

When you want to judge a person's thoughts or feelings about the deal, pay close attention to their body language while explaining the contents of the document or clauses. When the person tells you to go through a document, ask them to highlight its contents.

Tune in to their body language while they are going through the contents. It can be extremely revealing. You will know whether they are misleading you, trying to be manipulative, or genuinely interested in offering you the best.

Even experienced negotiators tend to deflect their attention on paperwork rather than focusing on people. They miss vital body language clues by not being alert and focused, and pouring over documents.

Chapter Thirteen: Recognizing Personality Type

" Tell me to what you pay attention and I will tell you who you are."
                    - José Ortega y Gasset

People analyzing is an intriguing and exciting process. It helps you unlock clues to a person's mental process that no one except he or she has access to. You will go into mental spots that were previously unreachable.

What's the number one tip when it comes to reading or analyzing people? I'd say, do not look for standalone or isolated clues. Watch out of a cluster of clues while considering the context.

People who are feeling cold may hug themselves or cross their legs and arms. If you're jumping to conclusions at stand-alone clues, you'll conclude they are not open to what you are saying or mistrustful. However, they are simply cold. This leads to a serious discrepancy between facts and your analysis.

You need to understand the person's fundamental or basic nature to establish a clear baseline for reading his or her behavior. Ask yourself questions such as, "Is this the individual's regular behavior?"

Do they generally display this behavior in a similar situation? What is driving them to act in a specific manner? This helps make your analysis more foolproof.

To make accurate assessments of people while reading them, look at a cluster of different verbal and nonverbal clues rather than heavily relying on a single indicator. Also, don't use people's situational behavior to determine their overall personality.

For example, a person may come across as increasingly aggressive or dominant while talking to someone who is bullying their (the first person's) child. This is because their parental instincts are at play. The person may not possess an aggressive or dominating personality. Thus, many a time, people's behavior is contextual.

Cluster of Clues

Look out for a group or cluster of clues if you want to read a person more accurately. For instance, if you want to establish whether a person is lying, look at his eye movements, his feet, his speech pattern, the inflection in the voice, the words or verbal expressions used, facial expressions, hand gestures, and more.

Observing a bunch of clues gives you a more reliable reading than catching single clues. When multiple clues point in the same direction, you will be more confident of an accurate conclusion.

Similarly, if you think a person is nervous, just because they are twiddling their thumbs, check for others signs of nervousness such as perspiration, hesitant speech, using gap fillers, and more. For all you know, the person may simply be restless or hyper-energetic by nature or plain bored. Avoid making the fallacy of jumping to a conclusion when it comes to reading body language clues.

If a person is stepping back when you confront them with a question, they could be lying. If their voice quivers while replying and they step back. They are more likely than not being deceptive.

However, reply in a quivering voice, step back behind and offer plenty of extra details, you can almost be certain they are lying.

See what we did there? We are just looking for more clues to make an assessment more accurate. For all you know, the person may be stepping back or shifting their feet because their shoes are uncomfortable. Based on this single movement, you may conclude that the person is lying.

It is pretty much the same when you are assessing someone's overall personality. Don't make assumptions based on isolated situations. Observe them in multiple circumstances before coming to a conclusion about their personality type.

The Four Temperaments Theory

The four personality theory is a proto psychological concept that talks about four primary personality types. It divides people based on sanguine choleric, melancholic, and phlegmatic. People with a sanguine personality are enthusiastic, socially-driven, and active.

Similarly, people with a choleric personality are impulsive, short-tempered, easily irritable, and quick to anger. Melancholic people are analytical, logical, and calm. Similarly, phlegmatic folks are serene and relaxed.

Most personality theories are a combination of two or more of these four basic temperaments. The extent to which each temperament is present in an individual determines their personality. Every person is a mixture of more or less these four fundamental personality traits.

Though the theory that bodily fluids influence four dominant human personality types was later rejected due to lack of evidence, a majority of personality classifications use similar categories for classifying personality types.

The DISC Concept

The DISC personality classification method is based on the idea that each person is distinctively different from other people in the way in which he or she thinks and perceives the world.

Everyone isn't similar to us, which is why we're left wondering what a person was thinking when they decided to do or saying something. Isn't it common to say things like, "Oh but why did she or he do that?" or "What was he or she thinking when he or she did that?"

What we are doing is evaluating a person's actions based on our personality, without realizing that their perspectives and thoughts are wired differently from ours. Yes, no one is like you. Notice how you can say something to five different people and elicit five different reactions from.

You said the same thing, but they all perceived it differently based on their personality or temperament. Thus you've got five different reactions to the same question. Think of it this way. There's a different chip fitted in the brain of every individual, which helps them perceive and process information in a manner that is different from others.

Take into consideration that different isn't in terms of good or bad. It is just different. Everyone is wired differently, which means someone different from you isn't necessarily bad. He or she just doesn't see things the way you do or vice-versa. A lack of understanding of this leads to plenty of heartburn and missed communications goals. It can lead to disappointment and unmet expectations.

There is a fairly simple and effective model for understanding complicated human behavior. It is referred to as The DISC Model of Human Behavior. It'll help you understand the minds or personalities of people to develop more rewarding people skills, which leads to more fulfilling interpersonal and social relationships.

Think how rewarding it would be to minimize conflict in any relationship and focus on productivity? How about being able to understand or relate to people more effectively?

The DISC model of human behavior is based on a couple of fundamental observations about people and their behavior. The first observation is that some people are more outgoing than others. There is an inner motor that drives people to "quickly go for the kill," while others have a more gradual pace. People are essentially outgoing or reserved.

The second basic difference is people are either people-centric or task/work-centric. According to the DISC personality model, we are guided by an external focus that determines our behavior. While some people are task-oriented or action-focused, others are more clued in to the people around them. Again, there's nothing like good or bad and right or wrong.

The four primary personality characteristics identified from the above discussion is: outgoing, reserved, task-oriented, and people-oriented. Now, each person possesses these qualities in varying proportions. Using a combination of these four fundamental personalities, there are four quadrants created to reveal four basic personality types, which have descriptive expressions beginning with D, I, S and C (hence the name DISC).

- -The first quadrant is people who are outgoing and task-oriented
- -The second quadrant is people who are outgoing and people-oriented
- -The third quadrant is people who are reserved and people-oriented
- -The fourth quadrant is people who are reserved and task-oriented

Let us attempt to understand each personality type.

People in the first quadrant are the dominant "D" folks who are outgoing and action/task-oriented by nature. They are always emphasizing on getting things done, achieving goals, accomplishing challenging tasks, and quickly getting to the point. They invariably make things happen. The key to forming a great relationship with "D" type people is results and deep respect for their authority or knowledge.

The "I" type person is outgoing and people-oriented by nature. He or she is heavily focused on enjoying people's company, socializing and having a blast. This personality time is focused on other people's opinions of them. They are deeply affected by what people think or say about them. Give them admiration, support, and recognition, and you'll enjoy a rewarding relationship with them.

The supportive "S" personality type is a combination of reserved, people-oriented folks. These people enjoy helping others and working in teams. They also find it gratifying to form solid interpersonal relationships. The best way to win them is by demonstrating a caring, friendly attitude, and offering sincere compliments.

The cautious "C" personality people are reserved and task-oriented. They are focused on consistency, reliability, quality, and accuracy. They are detailed and focus on facts. The key to developing a rewarding relationship with these folks is earning their trust and operating with a sense of integrity.

Connecting With Every Personality Type

Since each personality type has unique characteristics and areas of focus, it is important to understand how to connect with each type to establish more fulfilling relationships. Here are some well-researched tips.

Give "D" people the confidence that you value the end result as much as them. Be focused on the result while doing any task, and come up with a bunch of proactive solutions. They also appreciate when people come up with suggestions on how a task can be implemented more efficiently.

Respect their views. Don't challenge their opinion or views in public. Instead, offer solutions and suggestions gently in a manner that shows that it is beneficial for the overall task ahead. The "I" person is outgoing and people-focused. They are forever nervous about what others are thinking about them, which gives you a great opportunity to put their doubts at rest. Offer "I" people sincere compliments and positive/constructive criticism. Compliment their appearance, clothes, and external persona.

They are won over by admiration, appreciation, and recognition. Ensure you don't take them for granted and appreciate what they do. "I" folks are happiest when their efforts are recognized. Appreciate who they truly are, and play them abundant compliments and you'll dwell. Type "I" responds well to praise.

To connect with the "S" type personality, you need to have a friendly, caring, and approachable stance. They appreciate warmth, selflessness, and friendliness in a person. Since they themselves are naturally helpful and dependable, they expect others to be the same. Be there for them during tough times, and you'll win several brownie points with the type "S" folks.

To connect with "C" type people, work on winning their trust. They place a high premium of trust, loyalty, and integrity. It takes some time to be in their good books because they are very picky about the people in their inner circle. Bear in mind that winning them is all about being honest and ethical.

Conclusion

Thank you for purchasing this book.

I genuinely hope it has given you a treasure trove of insights into analyzing people's personality through tried and tested strategies, proven subconscious techniques and several practical, actionable tips. These tips can be applied in setting from business to personal relationships to social settings.

Whether you want to figure out the personality of a potential business partner during a business association or the suitability of a prospective recruit for the given job or the compatibility quotient of a potential date, this book is a handy resource for helping you analyze others effectively. If there's one skill that translates into success in the modern world, it is the ability to analyze people.

This allows you to customize your message according to the personality of the other individual to achieve effective communication.

The next step is to use the book and implement it in your daily life in small, slow ways to start with. Start by noticing people at the airport or doctor's when you have more free time.

Finally, if you enjoyed reading the book, please take the time to share your views by posting a review of Amazon. It'd be highly appreciated!

www.ingramcontent.com/pod-product-compliance
Lightning Source LLC
Chambersburg PA
CBHW071828080526
44589CB00012B/949